Kitchen Table Play & Learn

Activities and Lessons for Building
Your Preschooler's Vital Developmental Skills

Tara Copley & Andrea Custer

McGraw·Hill

New York   Chicago   San Francisco   Lisbon   London   Madrid   Mexico City
Milan   New Delhi   San Juan   Seoul   Singapore   Sydney   Toronto

Library of Congress Cataloging-in-Publication Data

Copley, Tara.
    Kitchen-table play and learn : activities and lessons for building your preschooler's vital developmental skills / Tara Copley and Andrea Custer.
        p.   cm.
    ISBN 0-07-146016-0
    1. Preschool children.   2. Child development.   3. Early childhood education—Activity programs.   4. Early childhood education—Parent participation.   5. Education, Preschool—Parent participation.   6. Parent and child.   I. Custer, Andrea.   II. Title.

HQ774.5.c66   2006
649'.68—dc22   2005016738

For our precious children . . .

Through your eyes we have seen the wonder of this world around us and the joys within our grasp. We thank God daily for our beautiful children and the opportunity He has given us to assist Him in raising these special human beings. We love you, babies!

2 3 4 5 6 7 8 9 0 DOC/DOC 0 9 8 7 6

ISBN 0-07-146016-0

McGraw-Hill books are available at special quantity discounts to use as premiums and sales promotions, or for use in corporate training programs. For more information, please write to the Director of Special Sales, Professional Publishing, McGraw-Hill, Two Penn Plaza, New York, NY 10121-2298. Or contact your local bookstore.

The activities in this book have been designed and intended for children ages two and older. We strongly recommend adult supervision of all children participating in these activities.

This book is printed on acid-free paper.

ABCDEFGHIJKLMNOPQRSTUVWXYZ

Contents

Preface

When our children were barely two years old, somebody was asking us, "What preschool will your child attend this fall?" every time we left the house. At first we thought they didn't understand that our kids were only two years old—this was our time for training and parent-child bonding. So we were very surprised to learn how common it was for two-year-olds to attend preschool. As uncomfortable as we both were with the idea of preschool for such young children, we couldn't help but wonder if we were holding on to our kids too tightly. Were they going to miss out on an opportunity that other families were taking advantage of? Deadlines for enrollment were upon us, and we quickly researched reputable preschools in our area and prepared a list of questions to ask the administrators and teachers. It was time to make our visits.

On the way to our first visit, we tried to stay positive and talk with our children about how much fun school could be for them; unfortunately, we weren't very excited ourselves. The discussion in the car to and from the schools felt rather somber and forced, not our usual Tara and Andrea chatter. We finally admitted to each other that we weren't ready to send our children off to school. Our guts told us our kids weren't ready yet or interested in going to school, and we weren't confident they had mastered the basics that we were still teaching them.

Our husbands were not convinced preschool was the right decision, either. We were interested in seeing what the schools had to offer, but we didn't feel our two-year-olds were ready for the real world. They were still learning morals and values and were very young and impressionable: "Train up your child in the way he should go and . . . he will not depart from it" (Proverbs 22:6). We weren't ready to relinquish the training of our children to someone else, and exterior social pressure to enroll them in formal preschool was certainly not a reason to do so.

Still, we worried that our kids would miss out on something. At the preschool interviews we attended, we found some spectacular facilities, knowledgeable administrators, and pleasant interaction between teachers and children. We thought we might enroll our children for socialization purposes, but our children already socialized with other kids at various classes, church, family events, playgroups, and the park. We didn't find that the preschools were providing anything that we could not do from home; however, we did see the benefit of exposing our children to some classroom experiences. They needed practice with following directions, resisting distraction, maintaining focus, and developing skills in a more organized manner, and we knew these could be introduced at home. We decided to hold our own classes. All we needed to do was visit the bookstore and pick up a preschool curriculum book.

That solution ended up not being as simple as we thought. There were countless activity and craft books, but not much for a parent interested in providing a manageable preschool curriculum from home. So we brainstormed for ideas together and pored through countless books, magazines, and websites to plan our lessons. Planning our lessons was extremely time-consuming, but the benefits far outweighed the negatives. Because we've taught our children every step of the way, we've had the pleasure of witnessing those "aha" moments and were available to love them through the land mines. They developed a deep love of learning as they experienced some of the wonders life has to offer.

Writing this book was driven by our passion for parents and children to experience what our families did this last year. Our book not only serves as a resource for parents who are looking for preschool lesson plans, but also gives parents a tool to better understand their own children, which is an experience that cannot be described by words. Children are capable of so much. All they need is proper guidance, love, and encouragement, and they blossom exponentially.

A B C D E F G H I J K L M N O P Q R S T U V W X Y Z

Acknowledgments

The hard work of parenting pays off every single day. This book coming to fruition is the icing on the cake! We would like to thank a few people for the icing. First and foremost, we thank our children. To Caige and Maddie Mae, our firstborns: The overwhelming love we felt for you both and the desire to protect your tender hearts inspired us to create these lessons. We wanted to witness your first little steps down the path of learning. What a joy and wonder that path has been for us all. Thank you for teaching us as we have taught you. And to Ellie Jo and Cord, our second little blessings: The anticipation of your arrival encouraged us to keep track of these lessons. We knew that someday we would want to share them with you, and now here we are with a book. We've just begun the journey of learning and growing with our newest family members, and we know each step we take with you will be a complete joy.

We also thank Becky Laborde, our early childhood advisor, for all the wonderful information and advice she gave us at the start of this process. You gave us the confidence we needed to begin teaching our children at home.

Our family and friends have been very supportive during this endeavor. We appreciate and thank you for all your advice, encouragement, grandchild-sitting services, editing, and for never asking us to "hush up about the book!" Now go buy all the copies of this book you promised to buy!

Thank you to Meg Leder for seeing the potential in this project and to Michele Matrisciani for walking us through the process of producing a book. We hope we didn't drive you gals to drink!

We would especially like to thank our husbands, Chris and Scott. This project has consumed our lives for the last year, and what we are really wondering is what you have been eating because we certainly haven't been cooking! Seriously, it was you who first recognized the value of what we were doing with the kids and encouraged us to share it with others. Without your support, this book would never have flown from the nest. Thank you for listening, giving us great ideas, lightening our load when we were stretched too thin, proofreading, and giving us the encouragement we needed to keep going on this project. You are our rocks and we know it. We thank God every day that we share our lives with you.

Introduction

Why should I teach my child using your book?

The fact that your preschooler is a learning "sponge" goes without saying. Children's brains develop at a faster pace between the ages of zero and four than at any other period in their lives. We know that as a parent you want to make the most of this time. The one-on-one nature of instruction in our book provides your child with more academic experiences than he would receive in a normal preschool environment. For example, it is very difficult for even the most dedicated teacher with ten or more preschoolers to give each child the opportunity to perform a science experiment, work one-on-one with cutting, or do a complicated craft. With our lessons, your child will have the teacher all to himself!

As the teacher, you will quickly learn your child's strengths and weaknesses. When you run across a skill your child struggles with, you will have the opportunity to focus on it. Likewise, when you find something your child breezes through, you will be there to take him to the next step and challenge his abilities.

There is no class pace other than the pace you and your child set. This will greatly decrease your child's frustration, as he will never be "left behind." Nor will he ever be bored while waiting for other students to catch up.

Whether or not your child is enrolled in regular preschool, our book provides a superb way for you to keep track of your child's academic, mental, and moral development.

Kitchen-Table Play and Learn is easy to use and parent-friendly. We should know: we are parents and we used these lessons to teach our own children. You and your child will be not only learning as you use these lessons, but you also will be creating some great memories that will stay with you for years to come.

Is this book a replacement for preschool?

Not necessarily, but it is up to you. Our book covers the academic skills expected of a preschooler and more, so it could easily replace a formal preschool education. It did for us. It would also be a great supplement to what your child is learning in regular school. Of course, whether your child is attending a formal preschool or not you will still want to do other activities that are vital to a child's development. In addition to using the lessons in this book, you should continue singing, reading books, doing nursery rhymes, and playing games. Motor skills are strengthened through repetition, so encourage your child to color, draw, practice writing, work with play dough, and develop large motor skills by doing outdoor activities.

If I use this book to replace preschool, what do I do about socialization?

In looking back on our decision to keep our children home a few more years, our primary concern was just that—missed socialization. However, we quickly saw other opportunities for social experiences. Our children were involved in sports, various classes, church, family events, and playgroups. There was plenty of socialization, and best of all, we were there socializing with them. Their impressionable minds didn't have to guess what behavior was appropriate in a social environment, because we were right there to guide them through. Our children could absorb values and manners under our wings, without receiving confusing messages from other well-meaning parties. We felt that it was important for our kids to be well-grounded in their beliefs and values before sending them out into the world alone. Two years later, we see that our decision is really paying off.

What should preschoolers be learning? What does your book focus on?
Wow! That is a loaded question because our answer is, "as much as you can teach them." Still, our book focuses on letter and number recognition, letter sounds, logic skills like matching and sorting, strengthening of hand muscles through fine motor exercises, large motor activities, beginning writing, knowledge of themselves and their environment, and much more. If a child can learn that a pig says, "oink," then she can certainly learn that an *A* says "ah." If a skill is too difficult for your child today, try again next week. She may surprise you!

How do you test to make sure your kids are progressing as they should?
Before we began writing these lessons, we visited many websites, schools, and teachers to completely understand what preschoolers and kindergarteners should know and be doing. We used that knowledge to develop our skills list and lessons. We found checklists of skills on the Internet and at bookstores to evaluate our children's progress on an ongoing basis. We suggest other parents do the same whether their children are in a formal preschool or not.

How did you develop your lessons?
When we realized we wanted to teach our children preschool activities at home, we looked at any resource that could give us ideas about lessons. We found many great ideas, but since we could give our chil-

dren focused one-on-one time, we wanted the crafts and activities to have even greater educational value. In developing these lessons, we adapted some craft activities commonly used with preschool-aged children to hone in on the skills preschoolers should be perfecting. In addition, we became well versed in the composition of crafts and activities, and we developed original ideas for each lesson. As a result, each lesson has well-thought-out activities with a developmental purpose.

What is the format of your lessons? Are they easy to use?

The format of our book clears the path for parents. We've done all of the tedious work for you, so you are only left with the fun of learning and exploring with your child.

- We have provided thirty thematic lessons.
- Almost every lesson teaches something about the alphabet, numbers, and motor skills.
- Each lesson has between nine and thirteen activities, as well as a review section at the end.
- The lesson usually starts by having you read aloud a book with your child. Then you move on to work with crafts, felt-board activities, games, experiments, and much more.
- We thought long and hard about the sequence of the activities to make the lessons exciting and engaging for your child.
- Each individual activity includes the skills being covered, materials needed, and step-by-step instructions. There are also suggested variations with some of the activities to increase or decrease the level of difficulty.

Are the lessons meant to teach one child at a time, or would they also work for a group? How long does it take to teach a lesson?

This book can be used in multiple ways by parents and caregivers.

- We chose to teach in a group setting where we traded off weeks of teaching and preparation. We met once a week for about two hours, during which we taught 1 to 1½ hours and let the children play for the remaining time. (The amount of time you spend working will depend on your child's attention span.) We enjoyed this method because we could share the teaching responsibilities and our children still got individual attention. Once the teaching parent explained the instructions for an activity, each parent would implement the activity with her own child. We also liked the group method as our children were learning to socialize while they worked. Sharing and cooperation became part of our weekly lessons. We started with a two–parent-child group and eventually worked up to a three–parent-child group. How large you let your activity group get is up to you. More children means more preparation, but you would be sharing teaching responsibilities with more parents, too, and would only have to teach once or twice a month.

• Our book could also be used by one parent. The lessons are written to accommodate this method first and foremost. Teach the weekly lessons as we did, in a 1-to-2-hour block, or spread the activities throughout the week, doing a few each day.

Is this book effective for working parents?

Our book is perfect for working parents as it provides a great way to stay in touch with your children during the hectic week. Dedicated weekly activities will guarantee that you spend focused time with your child and keep up with his academic and mental development. Your child will enjoy and look forward to participating in the activities with you, and you will have a strong understanding of any academic challenges that arise.

How hard is it to teach your own children?

For us, the hardest part was creating the lessons. A parent using our book will already have that step completed and save hours of preparation. Teaching the kids was never hard. Of course, some days were more difficult than others, but that is just a fact of parenting. We just pressed on, knowing that even on the challenging days, the kids were still learning.

Do your kids enjoy having "class" at home?

Our children have very different personalities, and they both look forward to activity day. Naturally, they have their own favorite activities, such as preferring crafts over games, and neither likes to get messy, but it is all fun and good. As we stated before, some days it is harder to keep their attention, but that is just the point. Their attention span is developing right along with their knowledge. No matter whether the kids have a great time or if the day is more of a challenge, they are disappointed when class is over and can't wait for the next week's lesson.

What have you learned from teaching your own children?

Where do we begin? We've learned that a parent, with or without formal training, can teach their children very effectively. We've found that involving yourself in your child's learning process gives you an even greater understanding of your little one and her development. We've learned that even bad days are good days. In the end, though, we think our greatest thought would be one of gratitude. We are just so grateful to have had these moments with our children, and we know that you will be, too.

Developmental Skills

Through the thirty lessons presented in this book, children will learn and sharpen the following crucial skills in language, mathematics, physical abilities, and science as well as social and other skills.

Language

- *Prereading.* Knowledge that print is equivalent to the spoken word and that a person moves through a book from left to right

- *Prewriting.* Holding a pencil, connecting dots, drawing lines, and understanding the value of print
- *Writing.* Writing letters and words using correct handwriting skills
- *Listening.* Developing attention span and focus through being read to, listening to instructions, and listening to others
- *Reading comprehension.* Listening to a passage to remember what was heard and understand the meaning
- *Letter recognition.* Recognizing and naming letters by sight
- *Phonics.* Associating a particular sound with a letter and learning to sound out words
- *Name recognition.* Recognizing his or her name by sight
- *Rhyming.* Putting words together based on their similar phonetic makeup
- *Vocabulary.* Adding to his or her list of recognized objects and words

Mathematics

- *Number recognition.* Recognizing and naming numbers by sight and learning that numbers have specific values
- *Measuring.* Measuring and comparing objects using various units
- *Logic.* Putting together puzzles and solving problems using thinking skills
- *Counting.* Counting consecutively
- *Rhythm.* Singing and playing music to a beat and learning to copy a beat
- *Shapes.* Recognizing and naming various shapes
- *Sorting.* Separating objects into groups based on differing attributes
- *Matching.* Matching objects based on similar attributes
- *Ordering.* Putting objects in order based on one specific attribute, like size
- *Comparing.* Comparing objects based on their value or size

- *Calendar.* Knowledge of passing time through the days of the week, months of the year, and years, as well as memorizing the months and days of the week
- *Telling time.* Reading a clock and attributing activities like waking or eating breakfast to a time of day
- *Ordinal numbers.* Order words such as *first, second, third*
- *Addition.* Understanding mathematical vocabulary and the concept of combining amounts
- *Subtraction.* Understanding mathematical vocabulary and the concept of removing value from an amount
- *Division.* Breaking an amount into groups
- *Patterning.* Creating or continuing a pattern using objects, colors, and so on
- *Graphing and charting.* Placing information into a chart or graph, and then reading it for information

Physical Abilities

- *Fine motor.* Strengthening hand muscles in preparation of writing, manipulation, and cutting; activities could include squeezing, pinching, peeling, manipulating, coloring
- *Large motor.* Strengthening muscles through a variety of large-body movement and exercise—like jumping, running, and throwing
- *Hand-eye coordination.* Improving the ability to coordinate body movements with the eyesight

Science

- *Colors.* Recognizing and naming colors
- *Classifying.* Putting objects into groups based on specific attributes
- *Prediction.* Predicting an outcome based on prior knowledge
- *Knowledge.* Gaining knowledge of a specific subject

- *Problem solving.* Applying prior experience and knowledge to the problem-solving process
- *Five senses.* Knowledge of sight, hearing, tasting, touching, and smelling, and learning how these senses are used

Other Skills

- *Object discrimination.* Using the five senses to discriminate among objects
- *Left and right.* Recognizing left side versus right side and direction
- *Memory.* Memorizing poems and songs, and remembering past events
- *Creativity.* Being creative artistically and in thought processes
- *Dramatic play.* Acting out a role, playing pretend, and other similar activities
- *Position vocabulary.* The meaning of *above, below, in, out,* and other such words
- *Map reading.* Reading, creating, and following a simple map

Social Skills

- *Life skills.* Basic skills used in daily life, such as looking both ways before crossing the street and fire safety
- *Self-awareness.* Knowledge of self, family, and the body
- *Following directions.* Following simple verbal directions
- *Cooperation.* Completing a task with another person's involvement
- *Sharing.* Sharing toys, time, and turns, during work and play
- *Public speaking.* Speaking in front of others
- *Giving.* Giving of time and effort for the joy and benefit of others
- *Sportsmanship.* Being kind during games, encouraging others, and being gracious in winning and losing

Know Your Child's Skill Level

The beauty of doing activities at home with your child is knowing his skill level and deciding how much of the activity he will complete on his own. We realize that a two-year-old participating in these activities will need greater supervision and guidance than a four-year-old. You don't want your child to become discouraged, so if something is too difficult, jump in with a helping hand. For example, an activity may require your child to circle a letter or object. If your child is not quite ready to draw circles, then have him identify the object but do the circling with him. The point is to keep things challenging but not make them frustrating. As time goes by, he will no longer require your assistance and you will have had the opportunity to see him learn before your very eyes.

If you find an activity to be too easy or difficult and you can't alter it for your child's skill level, you can go on to another activity. Each lesson has plenty of activities from which to choose. However, we suggest that you at least try each activity because your child may be more skilled than you thought.

Don't Panic!

Many of the activities in this book suggest having your child practice writing letters. If your child is not ready to write, don't panic! She isn't behind. The purpose of the practice is to prepare her for writing. Sit with your child, help her properly hold the pencil, show her how to write a letter by writing with her, and identify the letter and its sound. Before you know it, your assistance will no longer be required. Be prepared to set the writing activities aside for a month or two if she just isn't ready to write, because you don't want to pressure her into writing too soon.

Encouragement

Remind your child often how proud you are of him and how well he is doing. You will come across activities that are difficult for your child, so be sure to continue the praise for making the effort or overcoming a challenge. Make sure you correct, but do not criticize, because with lots of praise and loving encouragement, your child will master what was once difficult. Not only are you teaching your child preschool skills, but also he is gaining confidence and a love for learning with each activity.

Classroom Environment

The less distraction your child has, the more successful she will be. Designate a place in the house where you will do these activities, and make sure your child can comfortably do her work. She may need a booster chair and comfortable clothes. Turn the television and radio off, and put all the toys away. Make sure your child knows that sitting down to do activities means no blankets, stuffed animals, books, or toys are at the table. Commit this time entirely to your child, and make every effort to avoid things that will take your attention away from her. It will be difficult for your child to become distracted if your attention is devoted to her. This is precious one-on-one time with your child, so enjoy every minute!

You Are the Teacher

Remember that you are the teacher here and your child is learning to be a student. While participating in these activities, make sure your child is listening to instructions, sitting still, and not speaking out of turn. These lessons will help prepare him for appropriate classroom behavior when your child is attending school.

Letter Sounds

Schoolteachers often have to reteach many children how letters actually sound, because the children originally learned it incorrectly. It is a common mistake to teach children that *T* says "tuh" or *C* says "cuh." Say the word *cat* out loud. You hear a crisp "c" and "t." However, if your child learns *C* says "cuh" and *T* says "tuh," then when she is ready to start sounding out words she will think that *C-A-T* is pronounced "cuh-a-tuh." Avoid adding that "uh" sound when sounding out letters.

Resources

A wide variety of resources are available to you, including the following:

• *Internet.* Some of the activities in this book will require you to have pictures of objects or animals. We found our drawing skills to be less than adequate. Thank goodness for the Internet! Depending on what the activity requires, use the Internet to find coloring pages, free clip art, or handwriting practice pages. You will find your lesson preparation to be a bit easier when you don't have to draw freehand.

• *Teacher stores.* These stores cater to both teachers and parents. You don't have to be a teacher to shop at one. Look for one in your area as they are a great place to find teaching supplies such as paper, handwriting pages, calendars, clip-art CDs, toys, and books.

• *Libraries.* We start each lesson with an introductory activity of reading aloud a book about the theme for the day. If you are in need of a particular book, your local library most likely will have what you are looking for.

Lesson Preparation

Each thematic lesson has approximately ten activities and is meant to be taught on a weekly basis. It's up to you how you teach it. We taught once a week for about two hours, but you could do a few activities a day, teach over two days, or use another schedule. It's up to you.

Most activities have instructions for the parent to perform in order for the child to complete the activity. It's best to have your lessons prepared before class begins. Then when it's time to sit down together and do the activities, your child will not have to wait or possibly lose interest while you cut out shapes, look for paint, or figure out the best place to play a suggested game. Review the recipe and lay things out on the kitchen counter the night before, so you'll be good to go come class time.

Teaching a Group

Although you can have a very successful teaching experience at home teaching only your child, there are benefits to teaching a group. A group atmosphere is a great place for children to experience a classroom environment. They will learn how to take turns, share, raise their hands, use good manners with their peers, and take instruction from an adult besides their parent.

Another benefit of a group setup is accountability. Life keeps everyone busy, and it is easy to put off these lessons to do other things. However, if you make the commitment to your child and to other parents and their children to teach class and attend their classes, then you know it will happen. It's hard to let life get in the way when you have made a commitment to others to do these lessons.

Find other parents and their children who are interested in doing these preschool activities with you. We suggest keeping the group small because you have to prepare all of the activities for each child attending. Ideally, start by working with one or two other parents and their children; you could certainly add more children if you feel comfortable. Each week a different parent prepares and teaches the lesson to the group while the visiting parent works one-on-one with his or her own child. Not only will the children be learning good classroom behavior, but the parents will be responsible for preparing and teaching only once or twice a month.

Preparation Tips

• Don't sit for too long. Remember that your child is not only learning, but also acquiring an attention span. It works best if you split up craft time with reading on the couch, playing a game, or playing outside. Too much sitting makes for a grumpy child.

• You don't have to be an expert on every topic in order to teach these lessons. Share with your child as much as you know about the topic, follow the instructions in the lessons, and remember the library and Internet are great resources if you want to brush up on any subject.

• Sometimes children feel a little let down when crafts don't look perfect. It can also be tough for parents to let that crooked line sit where it is. Remind your child that her best is always good enough. Unless you are giving your child a little extra help, try to keep your hands to yourself. We know this is tough, but let your child be the creative one.

Teaching Tips

Keep the following tips in mind as you and your child work through the activities. Little adjustments can provide your child with a firm foundation to grow from.

• When reading a book, make sure your child can see the pictures clearly. Occasionally point to the words as you read so your child can see that you are reading from left to right.

• Always move from left to right when counting numbers or pointing to objects, as this prepares your child for the left-to-right movement in reading.

• Ask comprehension questions during and after you read books to your child. This hones her memory, keeps her attention from wandering, and allows her to actively participate.

• Whenever possible, have your child identify shapes, letters, colors, and numbers as they occur in the activities.

• Make sure your child knows how to hold a pencil properly so bad habits don't develop. Teacher stores usually sell rubber pencil grips, which will train your child proper thumb and finger positions.

• Each lesson has one or more letters for you to work on with your child. If your child is ready to write, we suggest printing handwriting practice pages (found on the Internet) for the letter(s) in the current week's lesson and letting your child practice all week long.

• When an activity requires your child to use glue, let him actually squeeze the glue bottle. This is a great way to hone his fine motor skills.

• Some kids are reluctant to get messy. Make sure your child knows it is okay to get glue or paint on her fingers. Encourage your child to get messy!

• Make sure your child always uses children's safety scissors with your supervision, and let him do as much of the cutting as possible.

Materials

The following listed materials are items used most commonly throughout the book. It's not necessary to run out and purchase everything on this list all at once. However, you will want to look at the materials for your current week's lesson and make sure you have everything. Before you know it, you will have all the supplies you need. Not only will you use them for the crafts in this book, but it's also good to have them in the house for a rainy day:

- Washable glue
- Extra-tacky glue
- Children's safety scissors
- Crayons
- Color pencils
- Construction paper, various colors
- Card stock, various colors
- Washable tempera paint, various colors
- Yarn, various colors
- Hole punch
- Small and large paper plates
- Craft sticks
- Pipe cleaners (chenille stems)
- Stapler
- Cotton-tip applicators (Q-tips)
- Paper towels
- Smocks or old shirts
- Masking tape
- Plastic measuring cups
- Food coloring
- Clothespins
- Paper lunch bags

- Black marker (permanent) or felt pen
- Flat kitchen sponges
- Felt board
- Felt or fabric interfacing

It's not absolutely necessary to have a felt board. Any activity listing a felt board as a material can also be done on construction paper. A felt board is very easy and inexpensive to make. You can find the materials to put it together at your local craft or fabric store. Buy a piece of felt that is 3 feet by 3 feet (1 m by 1 m). Cut the felt to cover the front of a foam or wood mounting board, and hot-glue the felt in place. Your child will enjoy being called up to the felt board to perform an activity.

Fabric interfacing is the best material to use for a felt board because it sticks well, it is fairly stiff, and you can still see through it to trace any pattern or picture. Fabric interfacing is used inside shirt collars to stiffen them and can be purchased wherever fabric is sold. You'll want to buy it in a medium weight so it is stiff but still easy to see through for tracing. Always trace or draw on it in pencil or permanent marker, and then color with color pencils or crayons. Washable markers tend to rub off. Great stuff!

The following materials are items that aren't used as frequently and could easily be substituted with another material:

- Precut construction-paper letters (check your scrapbook or craft stores)
- Glitter glue
- Glitter
- Chalk
- Various stickers (you can get variety packs at teacher stores)
- Craft pom-poms
- Google eyes (craft wiggle eyes)

The following items are things that you probably have in the house and would generally throw away. It's a good idea to save these items, though, as they are used in some of the craft activities:

- Jars (all sizes)
- Egg cartons
- Toilet-paper tubes
- Paper-towel tubes
- Shoe boxes

Lesson 1

A B C D E F G H I J K L M N O P Q R S T U V W X Y Z

All About Me

Featured Letters: Child's Name

Introductory Activity: What Makes Me Special?

Skills learned: Rhyming, listening, prereading, reading comprehension, knowledge of self

Instructions:

1. Read aloud to your child any book about being unique and special, and discuss his individuality based on his body, his personality, where he lives, and his family.

2. Say the following poem for your child, and repeat it so he can say it with you:

I Am Special

I am me and I am special. I am special, it is true.

The way I look and speak is special. The way I play and think is, too.

I'm so glad we each are different. It makes the world so bright and new.

I am me and I am special, and you are special, too.

Activity 2: "Me" Bags

Skills learned: Knowledge of self, vocabulary, public speaking
Materials: Any large bag, child's objects (photo, toy, book, etc.)
Instructions:

1. With your child, gather up some examples of what makes her special. Include a family photograph, favorite toy, favorite book, favorite snack, and example of a favorite color. Place the objects in the bag.

2. Then discuss the following questions with her:
   - What is your favorite thing to do?
   - What is your favorite song? (Help her sing it.)
   - What do you want to be when you grow up?

3. Have her present her bag and answer the questions for her preschool group or for the family one evening.

Activity 3: "Me" Books

Skills learned: Knowledge of self, vocabulary, prereading, writing, fine motor, phonics
Materials: Large paper bags (cut out the large sides to make big rectangles); stapler, yarn, or glue; scissors; old magazines and pictures; paper; crayons; family photo
Instructions:

1. Stack the paper-bag rectangles and fold them in half like a book. Staple, thread, or glue the "book" bindings together so the pages do not fall apart.

2. Let your child color pictures or cut out examples from magazines of his favorite things. Put one favorite thing on each page. Help your child write the name of the object at the bottom of each page.

3. Make a family page by putting a family photo in the book. Have your child help you identify and write everyone's name. Discuss what letter starts each name and the sound the letter makes.

4. On the last page, draw enough handwriting practice lines across the page for each letter of your child's name. At the beginning of each line, write a letter of your child's name.

5. Help your child practice writing the letters in his name three to five times each. Talk about the sound each letter makes.

Activity 4: That's My Name!

Skills learned: Prereading, self-awareness, name recognition, phonics
Materials: Felt board, black marker, paper, masking tape
Instructions:

1. Using large letters, write your child's name on a sheet of paper or print it out from the computer to make a name card. Make a few extra cards with your and other family members' names.

2. Put masking tape on the backs of the name cards and post them on the felt board. Ask your child to find her name. Talk about the sounds in her name and the sound that begins each name on the board.

3. Rearrange the cards, and repeat the activity until she can recognize her name.

Activity 5: What's in a Name?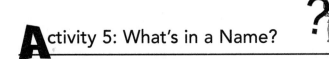

Skills learned: Prereading, prewriting, letter and number recognition, phonics, fine motor, rhythm
Materials: Construction paper, glue, various dried foods (e.g., pasta, beans, rice), crayon or pencil

Instructions:

1. On a piece of construction paper, write your child's name in large capital letters and his age.

2. Help him squeeze glue onto the first letter of his name. Let him do most of the squeezing, and encourage him to follow the outline of the letter.

3. Let him choose what dried food he will use to cover the letter. Have him pick up the food and glue it on the letter. Continue with each letter and number. Discuss each letter with its sound and the number of his age.

4. While you are working, sing the following song. Adjust the speed of the spelling section of the song depending on how many letters are in your child's name.

> *The Name Song (to the tune of "Bingo")*
> There was a mom who had a boy, and [Billy] was his name-oh.
> B-I-L-L-Y! B-I-L-L-Y! B-I-L-L-Y! And Billy was his name-oh.

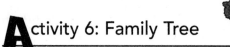ctivity 6: Family Tree

Skills learned: Knowledge of family, fine motor, counting, matching by letter, letter recognition, phonics

Materials: Large manila paper, crayons, scissors, family pictures (disposable), permanent marker

Instructions:

1. Draw and color a large tree on manila paper. Draw the trunk for your child and siblings, two large branches for parents, and smaller branches and twigs for extended family.

2. Write your children's names on the trunk; then draw apples on the tree to represent each member of the family you want shown.

With a marker, carefully print the beginning letter of each member's name in his or her apple.

3. Find photos of your family that you don't mind using in a craft, and cut out a small picture of each family member.

4. Explain to your child that a family is like a tree because each person is connected to the other. Tell her that today she is going to make her own family tree.

5. Show her the pile of family pictures, and go over who each person is. Start with the trunk of the tree and place appropriate pictures there. Work together to find the letter that each family member's name starts with, practice sounding it out, and ask her to match the pictures to the correct apple. You will have some repeat letters, so direct your child to the correct area of the tree. For example, "Jeff's name starts with a *J*. Put his picture on the *J*."

6. At the end of the activity, have your child count the members in her family.

Activity 7: Where I Live

Skills learned: Fine motor, knowledge of address, shapes, colors, life skills, prewriting

Materials: Small milk carton; washable paint; blue, green, and brown construction paper; glue; black permanent marker

Instructions:

1. Prepare your milk carton by painting its four sides the same color as your house and its angled top black. For grass, draw a narrow rectangle the width of the carton on the green construction paper. For windows and a door, draw two small squares on blue paper and one rectangle on brown paper.

2. Have your child cut out the shapes from the construction paper.

3. Have your child find the green rectangle and glue it to the bottom edge of the house for grass. Continue with the blue squares and brown rectangle.

4. Talk with your child about your house and how others can find it if they want to visit you. Lead him to understand that you have an address and that your address sets your home apart from other homes. You may even want to go outside and look at your house number and those of your neighbors. Help your child write his address on the grass of his milk-carton house with the marker.

5. This is also a great time to make up a little tune for your address for you to sing every time you drive up to your house. Doing this will help your child learn his address.

Activity 8: Body Outline Buddy

Skills learned: Fine and large motor, self-awareness, letter and number recognition, phonics, logic, knowledge of body parts, creativity, writing, name recognition

Materials: Butcher paper (long enough for child to stretch out on), crayons, pencil, yarn or pipe cleaners, mirror, plastic letters (refrigerator magnets work well), children's safety scissors, glue, fabric or felt (optional)

Instructions:

1. Have your child lie down on the butcher paper. Trace her outline onto the paper.

2. Let her help decide how to decorate the body outline. Discuss each item as you draw it in or make it. Where are the eyes going to go? How can we make your hair? What color are your eyes? Let her look in a mirror as she chooses how to decorate her body outline buddy. You can use yarn for hair. Have your child color the clothes to match her own or use real fabric or felt for the clothes.

3. Help her write her name and age with a crayon on the chest of the body outline buddy.

4. When the body outline is done, you may cut it out or assist your child in doing so.

5. Now give your child a stack of letters to correspond with the beginning letter of each body part. Ask her to find the *A* and put it on her buddy's ankle. Do the same with *F* for fingers, *H* for hair, *E* for elbow, *L* for leg, and so on.

6. Tape the body outline buddy to a wall, and take a picture of it with your child. It's a great memory! Later you can cut the body outline into pieces and use it as a puzzle.

7. Recite the following rhyme:

> *I Have Ten Fingers (to the tune of "Twinkle, Twinkle, Little Star")*
> I have ten fingers, I have ten toes.
> I have two ears and just one nose.
> I have a tongue and also teeth.
> I chomp with them so I can eat.
> I have two hands to clap for you.
> And with my legs, I jump up, too.

Activity 9: All Around the Body Parts

Skills learned: Large motor, listening, following directions, matching, knowledge of body parts

Materials: Large construction paper, crayons or markers, music, music player, masking tape

Instructions:

1. Draw the following groups of shapes (body-part shadows) on individual pieces of large construction paper:

- Child-sized face at the top, an outline of a right hand to the right, and a small circle the size of your elbow to the left

- An outline of a left hand to the left, an outline of a right hand to the right, and two circles stuck together in the middle (representing the child's rear end)
- Two elbow-sized circles at the top of the paper and two knee-sized circles at the bottom of the paper
- Outlines of the left and right feet at the bottom of the paper and of the left and right hands at the top
- A right ear at the top and an outline of a left hand to the left

2. Lay the pieces of construction paper in a circle on the floor with the body parts facing up.

3. Have your child walk around the paper circle while you play some music. When you stop the music, your child must quickly go stand in front of the piece of construction paper she is closest to. She should then touch her matching body parts to the shadows on the paper. For example, she would touch her face to the face outline, her right hand to the outline of the right hand, and her left elbow to the elbow outline.

4. When your child has matched her body parts to the shadows, stand up and play again. You can play this with a group of children. Older children can play an elimination game where the slowest child is out. Younger children can simply continue to move around and try again. It is great fun!

 Activity 10: Hula Hoop Game

Skills learned: Listening, large motor, self-awareness, following directions, rhyming

Materials: 1 hula hoop per child or a circle drawn on the ground with chalk

Instructions:

1. Lay the hula hoop on the ground in front of your child or draw a chalk circle.

2. Tell your child that when he hears his name he should jump *into* the hula hoop, and when he hears his age he should jump *out* of the hula hoop. Explain that he should jump with his *feet together*. This is tricky for youngsters.

3. Recite the following rhyme, and call out various names and ages when indicated.

The Hula Hoop Rhyme

Your ears are open, and I see your grin,

When you hear your name, you jump in! (Say a few names, including your child's.)

Your ears are open, so I don't have to shout.

When you hear your age, you jump out! (Say a few ages, including your child's.)

Here comes the tricky part,

Listen! Please do!

Name . . . *in*! Age . . . *out*!

The joke is on you! (Say various names and ages, including your child's, but mix them up.)

Review Time

- What makes you special?
- Can you name five different parts of your body?
- What letters are in your name?
- Can you sing the "Name Song" (to the tune of "Bingo") with me to spell your name?
- Can you sing a song with me about our address?
- What was your favorite part of the lesson? Mine was . . .

Lesson 2

A B C D E F G H I J K L M N O P Q R S T U V W X Y Z

School Days

Featured Letters: B, C, P, and S

Introductory Activity: School Book

Skills learned: Listening, prereading, knowledge of school, reading comprehension

Instructions:

1. Read aloud a book of your choice about school, and ask your child some comprehension questions about what you just read.

2. Discuss what children do at school, what they take with them, how they get there, and other similar questions.

Activity 2: Let's Ride to School

Skills learned: Large motor, dramatic play, letter recognition and phonics (*B*, *S*), rhythm

Materials: Large refrigerator box, sheet of cardboard, or yellow butcher paper; yellow paint; black permanent marker; scissors or knife for cutting the cardboard (to be used *only* by parent); yellow construction paper; masking tape

Instructions:

1. This activity is a little extra work, but a children's favorite! Cut the box, cardboard, or paper into the shape of a bus. Paint or color the bus. Get as creative as you wish. Cut out windows and a door that will open and close.

2. Write "__CHOOL __US" in large, black letters on the side of the bus.

3. Make five yellow construction paper squares, and write different letters on each, including an *S* and a *B*.

4. Tell your child that to get onto the bus she must first solve a puzzle. She must find the missing letters to complete the words on the bus. Your guiding questions will depend on the level of your child's knowledge. What letter makes the "s" sound? What does *school* start with? Where is the *S*? When she finds the *S* and *B*, help her tape the letters on the bus.

5. Now you both climb into the bus. Take turns being the bus driver and the student. While your child plays on the bus, teach her "The Wheels on the Bus" with the added verses as follows:

The Wheels on the Bus (traditional but adapted)

The wheels on the bus go round and round, round and round, round and round.

The wheels on the bus go round and round, all through the town.

The children on the bus know *B* says "b," *B* says "b," *B* says "b."

The children on the bus know *B* says "b," all through the town.

(Repeat the verse with *U* says "u," *S* says "s," and *B-U-S* spells *bus*.)

Activity 3: Pledge

Skills learned: Knowledge of the flag, patriotism, and tradition; memory

Materials: Flag

Instructions:

Teach your child how to say the pledge to the American flag or the flag of your nation.

> *Pledge of Allegiance*
> I pledge allegiance to the flag of the United States of America, and to the Republic for which it stands, one Nation under God, indivisible, with liberty and justice for all.

Activity 4: Calendar Fun

Skills learned: Calendar, logic, counting, rhyming, memory

Materials: Large perpetual calendar (bought or made), month and date labels (you can make these or purchase a set in any teacher store), holiday and event calendar squares (optional; e.g., birthdays, Christmas), white construction paper, felt board, masking tape

Instructions:

1. Make labels for "Today is . . . ," "Tomorrow will be . . . ," and "Yesterday was . . ." on your white paper.

2. Use tape to display your calendar and the months on a wall or felt board. Discuss the calendar in as much detail as your child is ready to handle. Show her what today is, yesterday was, and tomorrow will be. Talk about events and weather for the current month. Leave the calendar up year-round to discuss it daily, and use it to display events and holidays.

3. Teach your child the following song and poem to help her learn the months of the year and the days of the week. Point to each word as you say it.

The Month Song (to the tune of "If You're Happy and You Know It")
January, February, March,
(Clap, clap!)
April, May, June, July,
(Clap, clap!)
August and September,
October and November,
December! Then we tell the year good-bye!
(Clap, clap!)

Days of the Week Poem
Sunday! Monday! Tuesday, too!
Wednesday! Thursday! Peek-a-boo!
Friday! Saturday! So much fun.
Now a new week has begun.

Activity 5: School Supplies Treasure Hunt

Skills learned: Letter recognition and phonics (*B*, *C*, *P*, *S*), logic, following directions, matching, writing

Materials: Pencil bag or box, child's thick pencil, package of loose-leaf paper or notepad, box of crayons, children's safety scissors, construction paper, shoulder bag or backpack, large manila paper, black marker

Instructions:

1. Lay the pencil box, pencil, scissors, crayon box, and paper on the large manila paper. Trace around each object. Shade each traced picture to create object shadows.

2. On the back of the paper, write a handwriting practice line with a sample letter *S* at the beginning.

3. Cut out squares from the construction paper. Write the letters *B*, *C*, *P*, *P*, and *S* on the squares. The letters stand for *box, paper, pencil, crayons,* and *scissors*.

4. Hide your child's school supplies around the house, and tape the beginning letter of each school-supply item in plain sight nearby its hiding place.

5. Tell your child that she must have school supplies to go to school. Explain that throughout the house, each of her school-supply items is hidden next to the letter it starts with. For example, tell her she has to find her pencil. Ask her what sound and letter *pencil* starts with, or simply tell her that *pencil* begins with a *P*. Have her find the letter and the school-supply item hidden nearby.

6. Now show her the shadow page, and have her lay each item on the paper, matching the item to the shadow.

7. Have her turn the paper over and practice writing her *S*s. Review that *supplies* starts with the letter *S*.

Activity 6: How Many Children Are in the Schoolhouse?

Skills learned: Counting, number recognition, fine motor
Materials: Construction paper, scissors
Instructions:

1. Cut out four or five schoolhouses from the construction paper, and write a different number on each. Also cut out enough children to "fill" each schoolhouse based on the numbers you wrote, plus two extras to increase difficulty.

2. Give your child the schoolhouses and children. Tell your child that each schoolhouse can hold the number of students written on it. Have her place the correct number of students on each schoolhouse.

Activity 7: Lunch-Box Art

Skills learned: Fine motor, colors, shapes, letter recognition, name recognition

Materials: Plain cloth or plastic lunch box; fabric paint, puff paint, or paint pens

Instructions:

1. Explain to your child that students take lunches to school in a lunch box.

2. Have her decorate her lunch box with her name, shapes, letters, numbers, a picture of a favorite object, and other designs. Discuss colors as you go. Now you have a fun lunch box for outings.

Activity 8: Crayon-Sorting Race

Skills learned: Sorting by color, fine motor, hand–eye coordination

Materials: Plastic lazy Susan or turntable, 7 or more plastic cups or empty soup cans (with the paper peeled off and all sharp edges removed), paint or construction paper, crayons

Instructions:

1. Paint the cups or cans, or cover them with construction paper, so you have one of each color you are using. There should be a colored cup or can to match each crayon. Glue the cups onto a lazy Susan.

2. Give your child the crayons, and have her sort them into the matching cups.

Activity 9: Pizza Math

Skills learned: Counting, fine motor, knowledge of healthy food, fractions, prereading, following directions

Materials: Ready-to-eat pizza crust, English muffin, or hamburger bun; marinara sauce; cheese; pizza toppings; side dishes (e.g., crackers, apple slices, animal crackers, milk); index card; child-safe knife

Instructions:

1. Create an illustrated recipe index card with a picture of each ingredient, its name, and the amount used. For example, write "4 mushrooms" and draw four mushrooms. Use numbers your child is working on.

2. Assist your child in reading the recipe card to make her lunch. Let her do the work: spread the pizza sauce, sprinkle the cheese, count out toppings, and so on.

3. Toast or cook your child's pizza and let it cool.

4. Before eating, help your child cut her pizza into fractions such as halves or fourths.

5. You can provide a drink or let your child measure it out—for example, ½ cup (0.12 L) milk.

6. Enjoy your lunch, and don't forget to discuss eating a balanced diet.

Activity 10: Recess

Skills learned: Large motor, following directions, cooperation, hand-eye coordination

Materials: Rope

Instructions:

1. Follow the Leader. Knot a rope every 3 feet (1 m). Each participant holds a knot in the rope and takes turns being the leader. Followers follow the leader and do as the leader does.

2. Duck, Duck, Goose. Have the participants sit in a circle. The child who is IT walks around the circle and pats each child on the head. With each pat she says, "Duck." At some point she pats a child and says, "Goose." The goose must chase the child who is IT around the circle. If the child who is IT gets back to the goose's seat without being caught, then the second child becomes IT.

eview Time

- Can you find the letters *B*, *C*, *P*, and *S* in our activities?
- Can you sing "The Month Song" and the "Days of the Week Poem" with me?
- Can you recite the Pledge of Allegiance?
- What sound does *B* as in *bus* make?
- How do you make a pizza?
- How do you read a recipe card?
- What was your favorite activity in this lesson? Mine was . . .

Lesson 3

Ocean

Featured Letters: F, J, O, S, and W

Introductory Activity: Ocean Book

Skills learned: Prereading, familiarity with the ocean and what lives in the ocean, reading comprehension, listening

Instructions:

1. Read aloud a book about the ocean, and ask your child some comprehension questions about what you just read. Encourage your child to discuss the different creatures he thinks are in the ocean.

2. If you have a globe or a map, point out the oceans for your child.

Activity 2: Counting Oyster Pearls

Skills learned: Knowledge of oysters, fine motor, counting, matching

Materials: Felt board, scissors, felt (brown, white), black marker, hole punch, white printer paper

Instructions:

1. Cut ten oysters out of the brown felt, or use clip art. Use the black marker to write the numbers 1–10 on the oysters, each oyster with its own number.

2. Cut or use the hole punch to make 55 white felt circles to be used as pearls.

3. Place the oysters across the top of your felt board.

4. Explain that oysters live in the ocean and that small pieces of sand get trapped in an oyster and eventually turn into a pearl. Show her a craft pearl if you have one handy.

5. Have your child count the number of pearls for each oyster (e.g., number one oyster has one pearl, number two oyster has two pearls), and place the appropriate number of pearls under the corresponding numbered oyster.

Variation:

1. Group the felt pearls in a set of ten, a set of nine, a set of eight, and so on.

2. Give the numbered oysters to your child, and have her match the numbered oysters with the appropriate sets of pearls.

Activity 3: Jellyfish *Js*

Skills learned: Letter recognition and phonics (*J*), writing, fine motor, counting, knowledge of jellyfish, measurement

Materials: Paper plate, crepe paper, glue, children's safety scissors (optional), pencil

Instructions:

1. Have your child cut a paper plate in half.

2. Draw a handwriting practice line on the paper plate and a sample letter *J*.

3. Make sure your child knows that *J* stands for *jellyfish*, and have him sound out the letter *J*. Have your child practice writing his *J*s on the handwriting practice line.

4. Give the crepe paper to your child, and have him cut or tear a piece that is the same length as his forearm.

5. Have him measure as many same-sized additional pieces of crepe paper as he would like. These are the jellyfish tentacles.

6. Have him count the tentacles and glue them onto the straight edge of the paper plate. Now he has his own jellyfish.

Activity 4: Paper-Plate Whale

Skills learned: Fine and large motor, knowledge of whales, letter recognition and phonics (*W*), color recognition, patterns, writing

Materials: 1 paper plate, glue and water for glue mixture, blue tissue paper (various shades), children's safety scissors, 1 button, 1 dowel or craft stick

Instructions:

1. Mix 1 tablespoon (15 mL) glue and 2 tablespoons (30 mL) water for glue mixture.

2. Explain that whales live in the ocean and they are very large.

3. Explain that *W* stands for *whale*, and have your child sound out the letter *W*.

4. Draw a handwriting practice line and a sample letter *W* on the back of the paper plate. Have your child practice writing her *W*s on the handwriting practice line.

5. Help your child cut out a wedge (about 2 to 3 inches wide [5 to 7 cm]) from the outer part of the paper plate. The opening is the mouth. Save the wedge.

6. Have your child glue the small end of the wedge onto the paper plate, opposite the mouth. This is the whale's tail.

7. Draw a small half circle at the top of the plate, and have your child cut it out. This is the whale's blowhole.

8. Let your child paint the glue mixture onto the whale.

9. Give your child different shades of blue tissue-paper squares so she can put them on the glue. Let her glue some tissue-paper strips to the blowhole as water.

10. Glue the button on as an eye.

11. Glue the dowel or craft stick to the back of the whale so your child can hold it.

12. After the whale dries, let your child show you how a whale swims.

Variation:

1. For a greater challenge, have your child glue the tissue paper into different patterns.

2. To enhance your child's fine motor skills, use buttons, sequins, dried beans, or other small decorative items to make patterns on top of the tissue paper.

Activity 5: Bumpy Starfish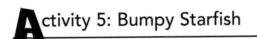

Skills learned: Letter recognition and phonics (*S*), counting, texture, fine motor, knowledge of starfish, writing

Materials: 1 sheet of construction paper, glue, oatmeal

Instructions:

1. Trace or draw five starfish on the construction paper.

2. Explain that starfish live in the ocean and they feel bumpy.

3. Have him count the five arms of a starfish.

4. Explain that *starfish* starts with the letter *S*. Then sound out the letter and have him repeat it.

5. Draw a practice handwriting line and a sample *S* on the bottom of the construction paper (with the starfish). Have your child practice writing *S*s on the handwriting practice line.

6. Let your child apply glue to the surface of each starfish.

7. Show your child how to pinch small amounts of oatmeal and place them on the glue. Let him do the same. Shake off the excess.

8. After the glue dries, he'll have some bumpy starfish to touch.

Activity 6: Fish Scales

Skills learned: Fine motor, knowledge of fish, letter recognition and phonics (*F*), writing

Materials: 1 sheet of construction paper, 1 unsharpened pencil with unused eraser, ink pad (washable ink)

Instructions:

1. Draw or trace the outline of a fish on the construction paper.

2. Explain that fish have scales. Also explain that *fish* starts with the letter *F*. Sound out the letter, and have your child repeat it.

3. Let your child dip the pencil eraser into the inkpad and stamp the fish until it is well covered with scales.

4. Draw a handwriting practice line and a sample *F*.

5. Have your child practice writing *F*s on the handwriting practice line.

Activity 7: Invisible Ocean

Skills learned: Fine motor, knowledge of the ocean

Materials: 1 white crayon, 1 sheet of white construction paper, blue watercolor paint, paintbrush

Instructions:

1. Explain that many creatures and plants live in the ocean. Sometimes it's hard to see these living things from above the ocean waterline. You will complete this craft to view the ocean from beneath its surface.

2. Use the white crayon to color fish, starfish, whales, seaweed, and other sea creatures on the white construction paper.

3. Let your child paint the blue watercolor on the construction paper to uncover the exciting ocean scenery.

Activity 8: Swimming Octopus

Skills learned: Counting, letter recognition and phonics (O), fine and large motor, writing

Materials: 1 paper lunch bag, crepe paper cut into eight 12-inch (30 cm) pieces, crayons, glue, children's safety scissors, hole punch, 1 piece of yarn (12 inches [30 cm])

Instructions:

1. Explain that an octopus has eight legs called tentacles.

2. Explain that *octopus* starts with the letter O. Sound out the letter, and have her repeat it.

3. Have your child count the eight pieces of crepe paper.

4. Open the paper bag, and let your child glue the crepe paper inside the opening.

5. Ask your child to count each leg. Help her along if she gets stuck.

6. Use crayons to draw a face on the octopus.

7. Draw a handwriting practice line and a sample *O* on the back of the octopus.

8. Help your child write the number 8 on the back of the octopus, and let her practice writing the letter *O* on the handwriting practice line.

9. Use the hole punch to punch two holes at the top of the octopus.

10. Have your child string the yarn through the holes and tie it into a loop.

11. Demonstrate how an octopus uses its legs to swim. Hold the string and pull the octopus up about 12 inches (30 cm) and then let it fall back down a few inches. Continue to repeat these motions.

12. Point out that the legs first are straight and then bunch up before straightening again. By making this motion, a child can see how an octopus really swims in the ocean.

13. Let your child show you how an octopus swims.

Activity 9: Gone Fishing

Skills learned: Large motor, measurement, concept of size (big and small)

Materials: Stick to use as a fishing pole, string, masking tape, bowl, construction paper, scissors, ruler

Instructions:

1. Tie the string to the pole, and attach a ball of tape to the end of the string.

2. Cut out several fish of different sizes from construction paper.

3. Use masking tape to mark where 6 inches (15 cm) is located on a ruler.

4. Show the fish to your child, and have him help you put them in order from smallest to biggest.

5. Then put the fish in a large container, and let him go fishing. You may have to help the tape stick to the fish by pressing it onto the first fish it touches.

6. When he gets a fish, have him hold it up to the ruler and tell you if it's bigger or smaller than 6 inches (15 cm).

7. If it's smaller, have him throw it back and fish again.

8. If it's bigger, tell him that he caught a good one and have him set it aside.

Activity 10: Saltwater Experiments

Skills learned: Knowledge of buoyancy, measurement

Materials: 8-ounce (237 mL) glass, water, salt, piece of a carrot

Instructions:

1. Fill the glass with water.

2. Ask your child what she thinks will happen when she puts the piece of carrot in the water. Will it float or will it sink?

3. Let her put the carrot in the glass and watch it fall to the bottom. Explain that the weight of the carrot in plain water will bring it straight to the bottom.

4. Ask your child what she thinks will happen when she adds salt to the water. Explain that salt will increase the carrot's buoyancy by making the water "thicker" and supporting the weight of the carrot.

5. Let your child begin adding salt to the glass, 1 tablespoon at a time.

6. The carrot will slowly rise until it is floating.

7. Discuss how the salty water and carrot relate to the ocean.

Review Time

- Can you tell me about some sea creatures you learned about?
- How many arms does a starfish have?
- Can you find the letters *F, J, O, S,* and *W* in our crafts?
- What sounds do *O* as in *octopus* and *W* as in *whale* make?
- How many legs does an octopus have? Can you count to eight?
- What happened to the carrot when you put it in salty water?
- What was your favorite part of the lesson? Mine was . . .

Lesson 4

A B C D E F G H I J K L M N O P Q R S T U V W X Y Z

Farm

Featured Letters: A, C, E, F, H, M, N, R, S, and T

Introductory Activity: Farm Book and Song

Skills learned: Prereading, listening, knowledge of farms, reading comprehension, rhythm

Instructions:

1. Read aloud a book about farms or farm animals to your child, and discuss life on a farm and the types of animals that live on a farm. Ask your child questions about the story you read.

2. Sing a farm-themed song with your child, like "Old McDonald."

Activity 2: Barnyard Shape Activity

Skills learned: Position vocabulary, fine motor, shapes, letter recognition and phonics (*F, A, R, M*), counting, colors, writing

Materials: Large manila paper; yellow, green, red, and black construction paper; several farm animal stamps, stickers, or sponges; glue; washable tempera paint (if using sponges or stamps); black crayon

Instructions:

1. Cut out the following shapes from the construction paper:
   - **Barn.** Large red square; large black triangle (to fit over the square)
   - **Tractor.** Green rectangle and green square as the body, two black circles for wheels
   - **Hay.** Three yellow rectangles

2. Give your child the large manila paper and the pile of shapes.

3. Name the shapes she should find to make the barn. Help her find the shapes, decide how to arrange the shapes to make the barn, and glue them on the paper.

4. Repeat this process with the tractor and the hay. Be sure to emphasize counting and colors when appropriate. For example, ask for three yellow rectangles to make the hay.

5. Using the animal sponges, stamps, or stickers, ask your child to find a particular animal and to put it in a certain location. Place the chicken *under* the hay or the cow *to the left* of the barn.

6. Now assist your child in writing the word "FARM" at the top of the page. Name and sound out the letters.

Activity 3: More Farm Animal Stamping

Skills learned: Fine motor, knowledge of farm animals, prewriting, counting, colors, sequencing and patterning (optional)

Materials: Several different farm animal stamps, washable tempera paint (various colors), manila paper, paper towels, crayon

Instructions:

1. Fold several paper towels, and place them on a washable or disposable plate. Squirt a small dollop of different colored paint onto each paper towel. These are your stamp pads.

2. Give your child the paper and stamps, and have her stamp each animal a specific color and number of times. Have her find the cow stamp, for example, and stamp it three times with the red paint. Continue with other stamps and colors.

3. Once the picture dries, give your child the crayon for fine motor exercises. For example, have her connect a chicken and cow with a line, put an X over a pink pig, circle a black horse, and draw a square around a blue duck.

Variation:

1. For a greater challenge in addition to the preceding instructions, use the stamps to start a pattern or create a sequence for your child.

2. Have her continue the pattern or copy the sequence.

Activity 4: Make Your Own Butter

Skills learned: Large motor, knowledge of making butter, rhyming
Materials: Lukewarm heavy cream, strainer, baby-food jar with a lid, salt, breadmaker and bread mix (optional)
Instructions:

1. If you have a breadmaker or like to make homemade bread, bake some and have it ready to eat once the butter is done.

2. Fill the baby-food jar about half full with the cream.

3. Close the lid tightly, and take turns with your child shaking the jar until lumps of butter form. This should take 15 to 20 minutes. Here is a rhyme to say while you shake:

> *Shake, Shake, Shake*
> Shake, shake, shake the milk up, please. Shake it left and right.
> Shake, shake, shake the milk up, please. Shake with all your
>   might.
> Shake, shake, shake the milk up, please. Shake it all about.
> Shake, shake, shake the milk up, please, and butter will come out.

4. Empty the jar into a strainer, and rinse the newly made butter with cool water until the water runs clear.

5. Add a little salt to the butter, and shape it into a form.

Activity 5: Eggs in a Basket

Skills learned: Creativity, fine motor, counting, number recognition, letter recognition and phonics (*N, E, S, T*), matching, colors (optional)

Materials: Large shoe box with a lid, brown paint, 4 muffin cups, masking tape, marble, 4 plastic egg halves, permanent marker

Instructions:

1. Tape the muffin cups to the inside bottom of the box so they lie flat. Use as little tape as possible. Paint the outside of the box brown to look like a crate.

2. Write one lowercase letter in the center of each muffin cup: *n, e, s,* and *t*. Write one uppercase letter on the top of each plastic egg half: *N, E, S,* and *T*.

3. Put a glop of brown paint in one corner of the box.

4. Have your child put the marble in the box and close the lid.

5. Let your child shake the box from side to side, causing the marble to roll around. Peek in periodically. When there are plenty of scribbles on the muffin cups, your child has made the nests. Let the nests dry while you work on another activity.

6. Darken your letters at the bottom of the nests, and remove the tape from the sides of the muffin cups so that they stand back up. Keep the bottoms taped down.

7. Give your child the eggs. Have her match the uppercase eggs with the lowercase letters in the nests. Help her glue each egg into its matching nest.

8. Have your child count the eggs, and then write the number 4 on the front of the box.

Variation:

A less challenging activity, if your child is not ready to match upper-case and lowercase letters, is to have her match colored eggs to similarly colored muffin cups.

Activity 6: Hatching-Chicken Sequence Cards

Skills learned: Logic, knowledge of hatching chickens, ordering, rhyming

Materials: 5 index cards, crayons or markers

Instructions:

1. On five separate index cards, draw a picture of an egg, an egg cracking, an egg with part of a chick showing, an egg with most of the chick revealed, and a chick completely hatched out of its egg.

2. Mix up the cards and give them to your child. Have your child put them in sequential order.

3. Teach your child the following song:

> *I See a Little Egg (to the tune of "I'm a Little Teapot")*
> I see a little egg as white as snow.
> It's so smooth to my touch, you know.
> When I reach to grab it, what do I see?
> A crack, and then a chick looking right at me.

Activity 7: Eggs Weigh-In

Skills learned: Comparison by weight, knowledge of weight

Materials: 4–8 identical plastic eggs, pennies, tape

Instructions:

1. Divide the eggs into pairs, and fill both eggs in each pair with the same number of pennies. This will make pairs of eggs that weigh the same amount. Divide the eggs into two sets so that each set has one egg of each weight.

2. Give your child one set of eggs. Have him pick up his eggs one at a time and find its match in the other set of eggs.

Activity 8: Cutting Hay

Skills learned: Fine motor, writing, letter recognition and phonics (*H*)

Materials: Yellow construction paper, crayon or pencil, children's safety scissors

Instructions:

1. Draw a large stack of hay on the yellow construction paper. Write a large *H* in the middle of the hay. Draw two parallel lines across the bottom of the hay for your child to write in. This is a handwriting practice line.

2. Give your child the hay drawing, and have her cut it out with her scissors.

3. Give her a crayon and have her practice writing *H*s. Talk her through the process (down, down, across), and be sure she goes from the top line to the bottom line. Discuss that *hay* begins with an *H*.

Activity 9: Pig Match

Skills learned: Visual discrimination, matching by pattern

Materials: Paper, crayons, scissors

Instructions:

1. Draw eight to twelve identical pigs, or print pig coloring pages from the Internet and cut them out.

2. Decorate pig pairs in an identical manner. For example, a pair of striped pigs, a pair of checkered pigs, a pair of pigs with a square on each, or a pair of pigs with four triangles on each.

3. Have your child match the pigs based on the patterns and shapes.

Activity 10: I'm a Little Piggy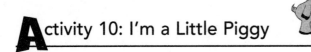

Skills learned: Large motor, dramatic play, rhyming

Materials: Paper or pink styrofoam egg carton, pink paint, glue, hole punch, yarn, black permanent marker

Instructions:

1. Cut out an egg carton section. Paint it pink if necessary. You may also let your child do this.

2. Have your child put two black dots on the bottom of the section for nostrils.

3. Assist your child in punching holes in the sides of the nose and tying yarn into the holes to make ties for attaching the nose.

4. Tie the nose onto your child's head, and let him pretend to be a pig. Make one for yourself, too, and be piggies together!

5. Teach your child the following song:

> *I'm a Little Piggy (to the tune of "I'm a Little Teapot")*
> I'm a little piggy, pink and small.
> If you stick with me you'll have a ball.
> I roll in the mud and play all day.
> And I don't have to bathe till the end of May.

Activity 11: Mud Writing

Skills learned: Fine motor, prewriting, letter recognition

Materials: Dirt, water, zipper sandwich bag, tape

Instructions:

1. Gather some dirt from the yard, and place it in the well-sealed zipper bag. The bag should be half full. Add enough water for it to become mud. Squeeze the air out of the bag and seal it. Tape up the opening, too, for extra security.

2. Discuss the many uses of dirt on a farm. For example, the animals lie in it to cool off and plants grow in dirt.

3. Give the bag to your child, and allow her to manipulate it with her hands.

4. Finally, have your child flatten out the bag on a table and practice drawing in the mud. To do this, she writes with her finger on the outside of the bag. She creates lines by displacing the mud as she presses on the bag. If there is a thin enough layer of mud, your child's drawings should show up when she draws with her finger. Have her draw shapes, letters, and numbers.

Activity 12: Feed the Chick

Skills learned: Fine motor, counting, number recognition

Materials: 4–5 paper plates, 2–3 toilet-paper rolls, yellow and orange paint, black marker, scissors, glue, dried corn kernels, tweezers with flat ends

Instructions:

1. Paint the paper plates yellow and the toilet-paper rolls orange. Cut the toilet-paper rolls in half; then cut out triangles from the opposite sides of each piece so that they look like beaks.

2. Glue each beak onto the center of a plate, and decorate the plate with the black marker to make it look like a chick's face. In the mouth of each chick, write a number that your child is working on.

3. Give your child the chick plates, tweezers, and a pile of corn kernels. Have him pick up the corn kernels with the tweezers and place the correct amount in each chick's mouth to match the number inside.

Activity 13: This Little Piggy

Skills learned: Large motor, following directions, listening, rhyming, knowledge of sequence, letter recognition and phonics (*C*, *H*, *M*, *N*, and *R*)

Materials: Ball (about 1-inch diameter [2.5 cm]), yard or meter stick, masking tape

Instructions:

1. Create an obstacle course for your child's pig by marking a path with masking-tape letters. Start with *M* for *market*, and then move a few steps and tape *H* for *home*. Continue with *R* for *roast beef*, *N* for *none*, and *C* for *cried*.

2. Explain to your child that the ball is a pig. Recite the following nursery rhyme:

> *This Little Piggy (traditional nursery rhyme)*
> This little piggy went to market,
> This little piggy stayed home,
> This little piggy had roast beef,
> This little piggy had none,
> And this little piggy cried, "Wee, wee, wee," all the way home.

3. Explain to your child that her piggy will do all of the things the nursery rhyme piggies did, but she has to guide it. Show her how to push the pig with the stick.

4. Ask her where the first piggy went (i.e., to the market), and together discover what letter *market* starts with. Have your child drive her pig to the *M* for *market*. Continue with the other letters until the last piggy goes home.

Review Time

- Can you find the letters *E*, *N*, *S*, and *T* in our crafts?
- Can you point to something red? Yellow?
- What is a farm?
- What types of animals live on a farm?
- What are some things we eat that are made or grown on a farm?
- What sound does *H* as in *hay* make?
- What was your favorite activity? Mine was . . .

Lesson 5

A B C D E F G H I J K L M N O P Q R S T U V W X Y Z

Dinosaurs

Featured Letter: D

Introductory Activity: Dinosaur Exploration

Skills learned: Knowledge of dinosaurs, prereading, listening, reading comprehension

Materials: Dinosaur book containing factual information (at your child's level), pictures of dinosaurs or dinosaur figurines, pieces of paper with dinosaur names written on them

Instructions:

1. Read aloud an informational book about dinosaurs to your child, and ask comprehension questions about what you read.

2. Have your child match your dinosaur pictures or figurines to the dinosaurs in the informational book.

3. Show your child the dinosaur sentence strips. Say each dinosaur name together, and decide what the beginning letters are. Have him match his dinosaurs to the names.

Activity 2: Dinosaur Song

Skills learned: Knowledge of dinosaurs, rhythm

Instructions:

Teach your child the following song:

Dinosaurs (to the tune of "Are You Sleeping")
Dinosaurs, dinosaurs,
Lived long ago, lived long ago.
They are prehistoric, they are prehistoric.
Their bones tell us so, their bones tell us so.

Tyrannosaurus rex, tyrannosaurus rex,
Lived long ago, lived long ago.
He ate meat and had big, sharp teeth.
His bones tell us so, his bones tell us so.

Apatosaurus, apatosaurus,
Lived long ago, lived long ago.
He was a great big dinosaur and was 70 feet or more.
His bones tell us so, his bones tell us so.

Stegosaurus, stegosaurus,
Lived long ago, lived long ago.
He had plates upon his back and with his tail could really whack.
His bones tell us so, his bones tell us so.

Activity 3: Dinosaur Colors

Skills learned: Colors, rhyming, listening

Materials: Construction paper (rainbow colors), scissors, craft sticks, glue

Instructions:

1. Cut out dinosaurs from the construction paper—one dinosaur for each color of the rainbow: red, orange, yellow, green, blue, and purple.

2. Glue a craft stick to each dinosaur, and allow them to dry.

3. Lay the colorful dinosaur puppets out before your child, and explain that you are going to read a poem with clues for your child to listen to. Based on the clues, your child needs to hold up the correct colored dinosaur.

4. Read the following rhyme, and follow the instructions:

> *I'm Looking for a Dinosaur (to the tune of "I Caught Me a Baby Bumblebee")*
> I'm looking for a dinosaur so keen. (Shade your eyes with your hands and look.)
> The color of grass his skin did seem.
> That would make him the color _____. (Let your child say the dinosaur's color.)
> There he is! You found him. (Have your child hold up the green dinosaur.)
>
> I'm looking for the dinosaur I dread. (Shade your eyes with your hands and look.)
> The color of a strawberry is his head.
> That would make him the color _____. (Let your child say the dinosaur's color.)
> There he is! You found him. (Have your child hold up the red dinosaur.)
>
> I'm looking for a dinosaur who likes to bellow. (Shade your eyes with your hands and look.)
> Bright like the sun is this old fellow.
> That would make him the color _____. (Let your child say the dinosaur's color.)

There he is! You found him. (Have your child hold up the yellow dinosaur.)

I'm looking for the dinosaur that flew. (Shade your eyes with your hands and look.)
He matches the sky—I swear it's true.
That would make him the color _____. (Let your child say the dinosaur's color.)
There he is! You found him. (Have your child hold up the blue dinosaur.)

I'm looking for a dinosaur in the loop. (Shade your eyes with your hands and look.)
He matches the ball you shoot into a hoop.
He is _____ (let your child say the dinosaur's color) and he likes to troop.
There he is! You found him. (Have your child hold up the orange dinosaur.)

I'm looking for a dinosaur in good shape. (Shade your eyes with your hands and look.)
His feet are the color of a nice dark grape.
He is _____ (let your child say the dinosaur's color) and he'd scare a snake!
There he is! You found him. (Have your child hold up the purple dinosaur.)

Activity 4: Dinosaur Match

Skills learned: Matching, phonics, letter recognition
Materials: Construction paper, black crayon, scissors, pencil

Instructions:

1. On construction paper, draw four or five different dinosaur shapes. Use the Internet to find dinosaur coloring pages or clip art if you don't want to draw freehand. Cut out the shapes.

2. Trace the outline of the shapes again onto a sheet of colored construction paper, and color in the outlines with black crayon. These are your dinosaur shadows.

3. Give your child the cutout dinosaur shapes, and have him match them to the correct shadows.

4. Now slowly say the name of each dinosaur, and either tell your child the letter it begins with or have him determine the letter based on the sound. Help him write the beginning letter of each dinosaur name next to the dinosaur shadows.

Activity 5: Dinosaur Cutout

Skills learned: Fine motor, writing, letter recognition and phonics (*D*)

Materials: Green construction paper, crayon, children's safety scissors

Instructions:

1. On the green construction paper, draw a large and *very* simple dinosaur for your child to practice cutting. Across the center of the dinosaur, draw a handwriting practice line. Write a sample letter *D* on the line.

2. Have your child cut out the dinosaur and then practice writing his *D*s on the handwriting practice line. Discuss that *dinosaur* begins with *D*.

Activity 6: Dinosaur Eggs

Skills learned: Counting, matching by number, number recognition

Materials: Plastic eggs, construction paper, black permanent marker

Instructions:

1. On the construction paper, draw five to eight dinosaurs. On each dinosaur, write a different number that your child is working on.

2. On the outside of each plastic egg, draw dots that correspond with the numbers you wrote. For example, if you wrote a 5 on one dinosaur, then one of your plastic eggs would have five dots drawn on it.

3. Give your child the eggs and dinosaur paper. Tell him the eggs are dinosaur eggs, and he has to get the eggs to the right mother by matching the dots on the eggs with the numbers on the mothers.

Activity 7: Dinosaur Fossil

Skills learned: Fine motor, knowledge of fossils and dinosaurs, large motor

Materials: Sand, plaster of Paris or baker's clay (available in craft stores), water, dry macaroni or other similar pasta, scissors, paintbrush or spray varnish, wax paper, a picture of a dinosaur skeleton (optional), white glue

Instructions:

1. Mix 1¼ cup (0.3 L) plaster and ½ cup (0.12 L) sand. Add ½ cup (0.12 L) water. Mix to a clay consistency.

2. Explain to your child that paleontologists are people who study ancient life. One way they do so is by digging to find the bones of animals that died long ago. The bones they find are called fossils.

Your child will create his own fossil of a dinosaur skeleton. Show your child the dinosaur skeleton picture if you found one.

3. Give your child the plaster mixture. Have him roll it into a ball and then flatten it onto a piece of wax paper until it is about 1½ inches (about 3 cm) thick.

4. Give your child the pasta, and have him press his pasta "bones" into the plaster to form the skeleton of a dinosaur. Help him make a head, backbone, legs, tail, and the rest of the skeleton.

5. Have your child brush white glue over the top surface of his fossil and let it dry. When the top is dry, brush the back with white glue as well. (You or another adult could also spray it with varnish.)

6. Once everything is dry, he can put his fossil on display or bury his fossil in the ground and have a treasure hunt to find it.

Activity 8: Dinosaur Puppets

Skills learned: Listening, creativity, fine motor, dramatic play, shapes, colors, rhyming

Materials: Construction paper (dinosaur colors), small paper bag (unopened), glue, google eyes, markers, white rickrack

Instructions:

1. From the construction paper, cut out multiple shapes that can be used for dinosaur facial features, such as an oval tongue, circle eyes, and triangle horns.

2. Have your child glue the shapes on the bottom flap of the paper bag so it looks like a dinosaur face.

3. Glue the rickrack to the flap edge, creating dinosaur teeth.

4. Let your child get as creative as he would like.

5. Have your child give his dinosaur a name and then slip his hand into the paper bag to make his dinosaur talk. You could also have your child make his dinosaur sing:

I'm a Scary Dinosaur (to the tune of "I'm a Little Tea Pot")
I'm a scary dinosaur, hear me roar.
I am going to frighten you, I'm sure.
I have got sharp claws and lots of teeth.
Now I'll growl at you and watch you screech.

Activity 9: Power-Packed, Torn-Paper Dinosaur

Skills learned: Fine motor, patterning, sequencing, large motor, colors, letter recognition, phonics
Materials: Construction paper (one or more colors), glue, large manila paper, dinosaur stickers or sponge stamps
Instructions:
1. Draw an outline of a large dinosaur on the manila paper. The stegosaurus works well because of his triangular plates.
2. Have your child tear small pieces (no more than 3 inches [7.5 cm] in diameter) from the construction paper. Discuss the paper color, and be sure to let him do the tearing.
3. Have your child glue the torn pieces inside the outline of the dinosaur.
4. Make a pattern with dinosaur stickers or sponge stamps at the top of the paper. Have your child repeat the pattern. You could also let him create his own pattern.
5. At the bottom of the paper, create a sequence with the stickers or sponge stamps—for example, stegosaurus, tyrannosaurus, stegosaurus, triceratops, apatosaurus, pterodactyl. Have your child copy the sequence. (Sequencing is great preparation for when your child is ready to start copying words.)

Activity 10: What Did It Eat?

Skills learned: Knowledge of dinosaurs, classifying and sorting, charting, counting

Materials: Dinosaur, animal, and human pictures or figures (try to find pictures with the mouth open); poster board; marker; dinosaur books for reference; handheld mirror

Instructions:

1. On the poster board, create a table called "What Did the Dinosaur Eat?"

What Did the Dinosaur Eat

Dinosaur	Carnivore	Herbivore	Omnivore
1			
2			
3			
4			
5			

2. Give your child the mirror, and have him look inside his mouth. Show him that some of his teeth are flat and dull and some are sharp. Explain that the dull teeth are for chewing food and the sharp ones are for tearing food. Discuss what types of foods can be just chewed and what types must be torn first. He should understand that meat must be torn while vegetables can be merely chewed.

3. Now look at a picture of a tyrannosaurus. All of its teeth are *very* sharp—so was he a meat eater or vegetable eater? Have your child look at the pictures or figures you found and determine what each animal and person eats.

4. Tell your child that *carnivores* eat meat only (*carn* means meat), *herbivores* eat plants only (*herb* means plant), and *omnivores* eat both (*omni-* is a prefix meaning all). People are omnivores, so people have teeth for all purposes. As your child determines the diet of each animal and person, have him place the picture or figure in the correct spot on the table.

5. When you're done with the table, ask questions: How many meat eaters did you find? Were there more meat eaters or plant eaters?

Activity 11: Dino-Size Me!

Skills learned: Knowledge of dinosaurs and measurement, comparison, counting

Materials: 55 feet (16.5 m) of yarn cut into a 50-foot (15 m) length and a 5-foot (1.5 m) length

Instructions:

1. Go outside with your child, and have him help you stretch out the 50-foot (15 m) piece of yarn. Tell him that this was about how long a tyrannosaurus was.

2. From the 5-foot (1.5 m) piece of yarn, cut a piece the height of your child.

3. Lay your child's yarn next to the 50-foot (15 m) piece and compare them.

4. How many of your child's lengths would it take to make a tyrannosaurus? Help him figure this out.

Activity 12: Dinosaur Stomp

Skills learned: Large motor, letter or shape recognition (optional)

Materials: Construction paper cut into 4–6 dinosaur footprints

Instructions:

1. Place a dinosaur print on the ground for your child to stand on. Now place another print within hopping distance of your child.

2. Your child must follow the prints around the room by hopping from one to the other. (You should tape down the prints so that the paper doesn't slip.) Try to get him to hop with his feet together.

Variation:

1. For a greater challenge, write a different letter or shape on each dinosaur print.

2. Have your child identify the letter or shape as he hops. See how fast he can do this.

 **R**eview Time

- Do dinosaurs live today?
- What did a T-Rex eat? Meat or vegetables? How can you tell?
- What is a fossil?
- Can you find the letter *D* in our crafts?
- What sound does *D* as in *dinosaur* make?
- What was your favorite part of the lesson? Mine was . . .

Lesson 6

ABCDEFGHIJKLMNOPQRSTUVWXYZ

Sports

*Featured Letters: B, G, and the Letters in
Your Child's Name*

▋ntroductory Activity: Team Shirt

Skills learned: Fine motor, prewriting, creativity, name recognition, knowledge of teamwork, letter and number recognition

Materials: Plain white T-shirt, paint pens or puff paint (puff paint takes longer to dry), poster board or cardboard cut to fit inside the shirt, pencil

Instructions:

1. Slide the cardboard or poster board inside the body of the T-shirt. On the back of the shirt, print your child's name with the pencil.

2. Help your child come up with a team name. Discuss what a team is and does. Help your child write the team name on the front of her shirt with the paint pens or puff paint. Keep in mind that puff paint takes a while to dry.

3. Let her decorate the front of the shirt, and then let it dry.

4. With the paint pen or puff paint, have her trace her name and write her chosen number on the back of the shirt.

Activity 2: Sports Equipment

Skills learned: Matching items, knowledge of different types of sports

Materials: Construction paper or fabric interfacing, felt board, masking tape

Instructions:

1. On the fabric interfacing or construction paper, draw pictures of sports equipment that can be grouped by sport—for example, bat and baseball, football and football goal, tennis racket and tennis ball, and soccer ball and soccer goal. You can also print clip art or online coloring pages.

2. Put masking tape on the back of all the pictures, and randomly display them on the felt board.

3. Have your child move the pictures around to match the equipment together by sport.

Variation:

For a greater challenge, place three sport items together, two that belong to the same sport and one that does not. Ask your child to identify what doesn't belong.

Activity 3: Bat-and-Ball Letters

Skills learned: Matching uppercase with lowercase letters or by phonics

Materials: Construction paper (white and brown), scissors, masking tape, black marker

Instructions:

1. Cut out white baseballs and brown bats using the construction paper.

2. Write uppercase letters onto the bats and matching lowercase letters onto the balls or letters on the bats and a picture starting with that letter on the ball.

3. Tape the bats on the felt board. Mix up the balls and tape them below the bats.

4. Ask your child to find the balls that match each bat and put them together.

Activity 4: Ball-and-Glove Number Match

Skills learned: Counting, matching by number recognition, fine motor, writing, letter recognition and phonics (G)

Materials: White and brown construction paper, black marker, large manila paper, glue

Instructions:

1. Cut out six white balls and six brown gloves from construction paper. You can use clip art or a coloring page from the Internet as a template.

2. Glue the glove cutouts to the manila paper. (Make sure to spread them around the paper to leave room for the balls.) Use the marker to write on the balls any numbers that you are working with and put the matching number of dots on the gloves.

3. Give your child the glove sheet and shuffled balls. Have him match the balls with the gloves and glue them on. (You could leave them unglued to play again.)

4. Write a sample G for your child, and then have him practice writing his Gs along the bottom of the page. Discuss the sound that G makes and that *glove* begins with G.

Activity 5: Bouncing-Ball Stamps

Skills learned: Fine motor, counting, shapes, colors, writing, letter recognition and phonics (*B*)

Materials: Construction paper, black marker, circular sponge (homemade or purchased), paint in any color, paper towels, plate, crayon

Instructions:

1. Starting at the bottom corner of your construction paper, draw a wavy or bouncy line across the paper. Write "__OUNCING __ALLS" at the top of the paper.

2. Make a stamp pad by pouring a small amount of paint onto a folded paper towel and placing it on a plate.

3. Give your child the circle sponge, paint, and construction paper. Have her sponge paint a specific number of circles along the bouncy line. Choose a number you are currently working on with your child. For example, have her place ten circles on the bouncy line to review the numbers 1 through 10. Let the paint dry while you work on other projects.

4. On the paper, write an uppercase *B* or lowercase *b* for your child.

5. Give your child the crayon, and help her practice writing *B*s all over the paper. Discuss the letter *B* and its sound.

6. Tell her that the title of her paper is "Bouncing Balls" but the beginning letters are missing. Help her fill in the blanks.

7. Have her count the balls again and help her write the number on her paper.

Activity 6: Ball Experiments

Skills learned: Knowledge of slope and balance, fine motor, prediction

Materials: Coffee can, wooden board that is 4–12 inches (10–40 cm) wide and 3–4 feet (1–1.5 m) long, cardboard, vegetable can, milk carton or juice jug (for height), tennis ball, tape or glue

Instructions:

1. Cut strips from the cardboard, and tape or glue them along both sides of the wooden board to form guides for the tennis ball to roll through.

2. **Slope experiment.** Lay the vegetable can on its side, and set the wooden board on top of it to make a slight hill. Let your child play with the ball and board, rolling the ball down the board. Discuss with him that to get a steeper slope he'll need to make the top of the hill higher. Now show him the three different containers you have. Ask him to pick the container that will make the hill tallest. Tell him that he is going to roll the ball down this new hill. Does he think the height of the hill will make a difference in the speed of the ball?

3. Have him roll the ball down each slope. Discuss why the steepest slope is the fastest. He should understand that the steeper the slope, the faster the ball.

4. **Balance experiment.** Turn the coffee can on its side. Place the wooden board so it is balancing on the coffee can like a seesaw. Have your child hold one side of the board, and tell him you are going to place the ball on the other end. Explain that he must keep the ball from rolling off the end by balancing the board. Let him experiment.

Activity 7: Marble Alley

Skills learned: Fine motor, number recognition, hand-eye coordination, following directions, addition, subtraction (optional), counting, prewriting, creativity, colors, shapes

Materials: Large shoe box, glue, construction paper (various colors), pencil or pen, children's safety scissors, masking tape, 10 marbles, large scoreboard (e.g., paper, chalkboard, poster board), decorations of choice (e.g., paper, glitter glue)

Instructions:

1. Trace the sides and bottom of the shoe box onto different colors of construction paper. Your child will cut these out to cover the shoe box.

2. Put a line of masking tape on the floor for the starting line.

3. Give your child the sheets of construction paper you traced on, and have her tell you what the traced shapes are. Have her cut them out.

4. Help your child glue the rectangles to each side and the bottom of the box. Let her figure out which rectangle goes where.

5. Cut out a small arch and a large arch from one long side of the box.

6. Help her write a $+1$ over the large arch and -1 or $+2$ over the small arch.

7. Have your child decorate her marble alley with a decoration of her choice.

8. Have your child get behind the starting line with her marbles. It will help if she lies down on her belly. Place the marble alley 2 to 5 feet (.5–1.5 m) away. Have your child push or flick a marble into an arch and declare the score. Record it on the scoreboard. Do this with all 10 marbles. When she is finished, give your child the pencil and have her make a tally mark for each point she scored and take a tally mark away for each point subtracted. Have her count up her score.

9. You can store the marbles in a felt or plastic bag for future play. If your child still puts things into her mouth, do not let her play with the marble alley on her own and be certain to store the marbles out of her reach.

Activity 8: Bowling for Numbers

Skills learned: Number recognition, large motor, hand-eye coordination

Materials: 9 toilet-paper tubes or empty water bottles, black marker, tennis ball, quarters, masking tape

Instructions:

1. Number the toilet-paper tubes or bottles 1 through 9. Tape several quarters to one end of each tube to weigh them down. Stand them up at the end of a long hall or on one side of an empty space in a room. This will work best on a hard floor. The tubes should be in consecutive order and placed side by side.

2. Give your child the tennis ball, and have her stand back about 8 feet (2 m) from the tubes.

3. Allow your child to roll the tennis ball toward the tubes to knock them down.

4. Set the tubes back up and have her aim at a specific number.

5. You can keep score by counting the number of times she hits the correct target.

Activity 9: Outdoor Olympics

Skills learned: Large motor, addition, cooperation, hand-eye coordination, following directions, measurement

Materials: Masking tape, rope, 1 potato sack or old pillowcase per participant, tricycle, 2 plastic milk jugs, beanbags, drinking straws, men's socks, tennis balls, timer (optional), chalk, tape measure

Instructions:

1. The following races can, for the most part, be played inside or outside. Players may race one another or in relays. If you have one child, let her race you or the clock. Make start and finish lines with masking tape. It would be safest to hold the races on grass or carpet.

2. Three-legged race. Have two players stand side by side and attach their inner legs together with rope or tape. When you say go, they must cooperate to walk to the finish line. This race could be done in child–child teams or child–parent teams.

3. Potato-sack race. Have your child stand inside a potato sack or pillowcase and hop to the finish line.

4. Tricycle obstacle course. Set up an obstacle course outside where your child can ride between tape or chalk lines, under folding tables, or around other obstacles.

5. Milk jug toss. Cut off the top of a plastic milk jug, but leave the handle. Have a child or yourself throw a tennis ball or beanbag to another child holding the jug by its handle. The child with the jug will try to catch the beanbag in the jug. Do this eight to ten times. The score will equal the number of times the beanbag is caught.

6. Javelin throw. Using a straw, demonstrate how to throw a javelin forward. Have your child throw a straw, and then help her measure how far the straw went with a measuring stick or measuring tape.

7. Hammer throw. Place a tennis ball into a man's sock and tie it closed to make a hammer. Show your child the hammer throw by holding the "hammer" out with one hand, spinning your body around, and then releasing the hammer. Have your child try the hammer throw, and then help her measure how far it went.

Activity 10: Game Day Snacks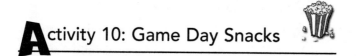

Skills learned: Sharing, life skills, shapes
Materials: Lemonade, round crackers, cheese, peanuts, candied or plain popcorn

Instructions:

1. Cut the cheese into squares.

2. Serve these snacks at any time during the day. Emphasize sharing and taking turns. Maybe have the child serve you, or the children serve one another.

3. Ask her what shapes the crackers and cheese pieces are.

Review Time

- Can you find the letters *B* and *G* in our crafts?
- How did we play marble alley?
- If you score 1 point and then 2 more, what is your score?
- Why does a ball roll down a steep hill faster than a low hill?
- What sound does *G* as in *glove* make?
- What was your favorite activity today? Mine was . . .

Lesson 7

A B C D E F G H I J K L M N O P Q R S T U V W X Y Z

Transportation

Featured Letters: S, T, and Y

Introductory Activity: Transportation Book

Skills learned: Prereading, listening, knowledge of transportation, logic, reading comprehension

Materials: Any book discussing multiple modes of transportation, pictures of several modes of transportation and their destinations (e.g., car and house, train and other state, rocket and moon, airplane and another country)

Instructions:

1. Read aloud a transportation book to your child, and discuss the different types of transportation and what they are used for. Ask comprehension questions about the story you read.

2. Play a game with your child by showing him a mixed-up pile of transportation pictures. Hold up a picture of a destination, and ask him which of the different modes of transportation would be best to use to travel there. Why?

Activity 2: Where Does It Go?

Skills learned: Matching items

Materials: Pictures of transportation items and where they run, felt board (optional), masking tape (optional), fabric interfacing or paper

Instructions:

1. Create pictures of different modes of transportation by drawing them on fabric interfacing or printing them from clip art or coloring pages from the Internet. Also create pictures of where the transportation items run—for example, airplane and sky, canoe and pond, ship and ocean, car and road, train and train track.

2. Cut out the pictures, and back them with masking tape if you use paper.

3. Randomly display the pictures on the felt board. Give your child one of the modes of transportation, and ask him to match it to the picture of where it runs.

4. Repeat with all of the matching sets.

Activity 3: Transportation Sort

Skills learned: Parent's choice but good for number or letter recognition, phonics, matching lowercase and uppercase letters, telling time, colors, shapes, sorting, listening

Materials: 4–5 small boxes (about 3 by 4 inches [7.5 by 10 cm]), construction paper, scissors, masking tape

Instructions:

1. Use the boxes to make a train engine and several cars. Staple or tape them to the felt board. Decide what skill your child will work on, and make appropriate cards. One set will be given to your child for sorting into the train cars, and the other will be taped onto the cars. For example:

- Numbers (give to child) and corresponding dots (glue to side of train cars)
- Clock faces with times and corresponding digital times
- Uppercase letters and matching lowercase letters
- Uppercase letters and pictures with matching beginning or ending sounds

2. Have your child sort his cards into the appropriate train cars.

Variation:

For simpler skills like shape and color recognition, put a picture of the shape or example of the color on the train car and give your child a token of some sort. Ask him to put the token into the train car with the rectangle, red square, or any other shape or color.

Activity 4: Traffic Sign Shadow Match

Skills learned: Matching, knowledge of traffic signs, prereading, writing, letter recognition and phonics (*T*, *S*), shapes, visual discrimination

Materials: Construction paper, scissors, markers or crayons, glue (optional)

Instructions:

1. Create 2-to-3-inch (5 to 7.5 cm) pictures of common traffic signs: for example, stop, yield, speed limit, and railroad crossing. The important thing is to look for different shaped signs.

2. Cut out the signs; then trace them onto a piece of construction paper. Color the outlines black to create shadows.

3. Discuss with your child what a traffic sign is. Give your child the shadow paper and corresponding signs, and have him match them by laying the sign on top of the shadow. He can glue these together or keep them loose to play again later. As he matches the signs with the shadows, be sure to question him about each sign's shape and color.

4. After your child is done matching, ask him if he knows what any of the signs mean. Talk about them, as well as about the ones he doesn't know.

5. Discuss what *traffic* and *sign* start with. Help him practice writing his *T*s and *S*s on the paper.

Activity 5: Traffic Light

Skills learned: Large motor, listening, following directions, rhythm, knowledge of traffic lights

Materials: Red, yellow, green construction paper; scissors; glue; craft sticks

Instructions:

1. Cut out identical circles from red, yellow, and green construction paper. Glue these onto three separate craft sticks. These are your traffic lights.

2. Have your child stand several yards away from you, and tell him that you are going to play a game called Traffic Light. When you hold up the green light, he should begin walking toward you; red light means stop, and yellow light means slow down. His goal is to reach you quickly or first. If he moves when the red light is up, he must go back to start.

3. Teach this song to help your child remember the rules:

> *Traffic Light Song (to the tune of "Bingo")*
> I see a light across the road, but what does it say-o?
> If you see green, then you may go.
> Please be careful if it is yellow.
> And when it's red here's what you do,
> *Stop!* If you know what's good for you.

Activity 6: Yield

Skills learned: Fine motor, writing, letter recognition and phonics (*Y*)

Materials: White construction paper, red crayon, black marker, children's safety scissors

Instructions:

1. Draw a large upside-down triangle on the construction paper. This is a yield sign. Color the edge in red. Draw a handwriting practice line across the middle of the sign, and write a sample *Y* at the beginning of it.

2. Give your child the paper with the yield sign, and have him practice writing his *Y*s. Discuss the sound a Y makes and that *yield* begins with Y.

3. Have him cut out the sign.

Activity 7: Tire Track Art

Skills learned: Matching, large motor, primary to secondary colors, letter recognition and phonics (*T*), writing, prereading

Materials: 2–5 washable toy cars (each with different-sized wheels), washable tempera paint in primary colors (red, yellow, and blue), large manila paper, paint bowls large enough to accommodate your cars

Instructions:

1. Prepare your own tire art by dipping each car's wheels into the same color of tempera paint and rolling the tires across a large piece of paper to make tracks. Wash the cars.

2. Show your child your tire art and the cars that made the tracks. Help him match the car to the appropriate tracks by looking at the track and wheel sizes.

3. Now help him dip the cars into a paint color of his choice and roll tracks across his own paper. Encourage him to use different colors of paint, and discuss what happens when the colors mix. For example, red and yellow make orange.

Activity 8: Shapely Transportation Mobile

Skills learned: Shapes, fine motor, creativity, counting, listening, logic, color

Materials: Construction paper, children's safety scissors, glue, paper plate, yarn, hole punch

Instructions:

1. Your child will make vehicles out of shapes. Decide what shapes are necessary for the vehicles you want to create; then draw and cut them out of construction paper. Write down what shapes you used to make each vehicle. You can make this activity simple or difficult. For example:

- **Train.** One large rectangle (body of train), one square (cab), one triangle (snow plow), three circles (wheels)
- **Car.** One large rectangle (car body), two circles (wheels), and one small rectangle (cab)
- **Airplane.** Two tall and thin triangles (wings), one long rectangle (airplane body), small squares (windows), and one small triangle (nose of airplane)

2. Give your child the pile of shapes and a piece of construction paper. Tell your child what shapes to gather for one vehicle.

3. Have your child decide how to put the vehicle together and glue it on the construction paper. You can also discuss colors at this time.

4. Repeat this process for each vehicle.

5. Have your child decorate a paper plate with stickers, crayons, and his name.

6. After the vehicles have dried, help your child cut them out.

7. Punch a hole in each vehicle. Punch holes into the paper plate, one for each vehicle.

8. Attach the vehicles to the paper plate with pieces of yarn. Hang the mobile to display.

Activity 9: Dot-to-Dot

Skills learned: Fine motor, number or letter recognition, prewriting

Materials: Printer paper, crayons or pencils, any simple coloring page of a vehicle

Instructions:

1. Draw a simple vehicle or find a simple coloring page of any type of vehicle. Place a piece of printer paper over the picture so you can see the picture through the paper. At each major corner of the drawing, place a dot on your printer paper. There should be enough dots to redraw the picture, but not too many for your child. Find a starting point; then label the dots in consecutive order with either numbers or letters.

2. Give your child the dot-to-dot picture, and have him connect the dots by following consecutive numbers or letters. Encourage him to make straight lines.

Activity 10: Balloon Car Race

Skills learned: Knowledge of wind force, fine motor, prediction

Materials: Toy cars of equal sizes that roll (midsize); masking tape; balloons; hard, flat surface; clothespins

Instructions:

1. Blow up the balloons to as equal sizes as possible, and then pinch off the openings with a clip. Tape a balloon to the top of each car with the open end of the balloon pointed to the rear of the car. Tape a start line on the floor.

2. Show your child the cars, and tell him that he will conduct a car race but he won't have to push his car to make it go. Help him line up his car at the starting line.

3. When you say go, your child unclips the opening of the balloon and watches the car take off. A friend or you can race a car, as well. Talk about what makes the cars move (the force of the air leaving the balloon).

4. Now race again, but fill the balloons to different capacities for each car (full and half-full). Have your child predict which car will go the farthest.

Activity 11: Road-Building Race

Skills learned: Fine and large motor, listening, following directions
Materials: Multiple wooden blocks, masking tape
Instructions:
1. Give your child a pile of wooden blocks. Tape start and finish lines on the floor, and pile the blocks up at the starting line.
2. Tell your child that when you say go, he must build a block road from the starting line to the finish as quickly as possible. Parent can participate, too, and make it a race.

Activity 12: Car Wash

Skills learned: Large motor, life skills
Materials: Bucket, sponge, dishwashing liquid, water, drying rags, car or tricycle, water hose
Instructions:
Help your child wash the family car or his tricycle. Be sure to emphasize squeezing out the water from the sponge, directing the

water hose, making the water spray, and making large circular motions with his arms to wash and dry.

Activity 13: Crossing-the-Street Practice

Skills learned: Large motor, life skills, rhyming

Instructions:

1. Discuss and practice with your child the rules of crossing a street. Teach your child to always hold an adult's hand in a parking lot or around streets. Remind him that he must stop at the edge of the street to check for cars. Look left and right and then left again before crossing.

2. Teach him this rhyme to help him remember the safety rule:

Crossing the Street
To cross a street you first must *stop*! (Stick out your right palm
    on *stop*.)
Now look *left* and *right*. (Look left and right.)
Very good, but look again for cars out of your sight. (Look left.)
Now you may cross, but hurry please, there is no time to play.
    (Cross the street.)
We want you to be here to cross upon another day.

Review Time

- What is the best way to travel to a friend's house? Another state? Across an ocean? To the moon?
- Can you find the letters *S*, *T*, and *Y* in our crafts?
- What are the rules for crossing the street?
- Why does the air from a large balloon push a car farther than the air from a small balloon does?
- What sound does *Y* as in *yield* make?
- What was your favorite part of the lesson? Mine was . . .

Lesson 8

A B C D E F G H I J K L M N O P Q R S T U V W X Y Z

Rain Forest

Featured Letters: A, L, R, and T

Introductory Activity: Rain Forest Book

Skills learned: Knowledge of the rain forest and its plants and animals, prereading, reading comprehension, listening

Instructions:

1. Read aloud a book about the rain forest, and ask your child some comprehension questions.

2. This is a great time to talk about the difference between weather in your hometown and in a rain forest.

3. Discuss the different animals in the rain forest.

Activity 2: Scaly Snakes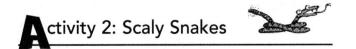

Skills learned: Patterns, fine motor

Materials: Construction paper, glue, large sequins (several different colors)

Instructions:

1. Draw the outline of a snake on construction paper, or go online and print out a snake coloring page.

2. Help your child put glue on the snake.

3. Help your child use the sequins to make a pattern of colors on the snake. You can either put a picture of a snake on the table for her to copy, or she can establish a pattern of her own.

4. When the snake dries, there will be a beautiful pattern and it will feel scaly—just like a snake!

Activity 3: Hidden Animals

Skills learned: Fine motor, knowledge of camouflage

Materials: White construction paper, green paint, sponge, rain forest animal cutouts (easy to find on the Internet), masking tape

Instructions:

1. Find several different kinds of rain forest animals online or in magazines, and cut them out. Make sure you cut the actual shape of the animal.

2. Help your child tape the animals to the construction paper. Make sure the tape doesn't show.

3. Have your child dip the sponge into the green paint and cover all the construction paper, including the animals, with sponge-print leaves. Make sure the sponge is small so your child can work on her pinching skills, which will help with writing skills.

4. Explain that the rain forest is very dense and many animals use the thick leaves to hide or camouflage themselves.

5. Set the painting aside to dry. Once it is dry, have your child peel the cutouts off the construction paper to see where the animals were hiding.

Activity 4: Animal Letter Sounds

Skills learned: Phonics, matching, letter recognition, knowledge of rain forest animals

Materials: 2 pieces of construction paper, marker, glue, pictures of various rain forest animals

Instructions:

1. Use the Internet to find color pictures or coloring pages of rain forest animals. Print and cut the pictures out. Make sure the pictures are not bigger than 3-by-3 inch (8 by 8 cm).

2. Cut out 3-by-3-inch (8 by 8 cm) construction paper squares. Glue the animal cutouts onto the construction-paper squares.

3. Draw 3-by-3-inch (8 by 8 cm) squares on a clean piece of construction paper.

4. Write the beginning letter for each animal inside the squares.

5. Show the animals to your child and help her sound out the first letters for each animal. Give the animals to her. Again, have her sound out the animal names and match each first-letter sound to the corresponding letter on the construction paper.

6. Help her glue the top of the animal square to the top of the letter square. When it's dry, she should be able to look at the animal, sound out its name, and flip the animal square up to reveal the letter it starts with.

Activity 5: Animal Action

Skills learned: Imagination, creativity, large motor

Materials: Animal crackers

Instructions:

1. Let your child pick one animal cracker and act out the sounds of the animal she has chosen.

2. If there is a group of children, let each child take a turn acting out an animal while the other children guess what animal the child is pretending to be.

Activity 6: Hopping Frogs

Skills learned: Listening, hand-eye coordination, letter recognition and phonics (*L*), writing, fine motor, rhyming
Materials: Beanbags or something small for tossing, green construction paper, children's safety scissors, pencil or crayon
Instructions:
1. Trace a large lily pad on the green construction paper.
2. Supervise your child as she cuts out the lily pad with children's safety scissors.
3. Draw a handwriting practice line on the lily pad and a sample *L*.
4. Make sure your child knows that *lily* starts with the letter *L*. Have her make the "l" sound.
5. Give the pencil or crayon to your child, and let her practice writing the letter *L* on the handwriting practice line.
6. Place the lily pad on the floor. Say the following rhyme to your child. When you say "three" in the rhyme, instruct your child to throw the beanbag onto the lily pad.

> The rain forest frogs jump from tree to tree.
> Then they jump to a lily pad, one, two, three!

7. Encourage your child to say the rhyme with you.

Activity 7: Toad Skin

Skills learned: Knowledge of toads, fine motor, distinguishing smooth and bumpy textures, letter recognition and phonics (*T*), writing

Materials: Coloring page of a toad, pictures of frogs and toads, glue, rice, crayons

Instructions:

1. Show your child pictures of toads and poison dart frogs (you can find pictures online or in books). Ask her to tell you the differences she sees.

2. Make sure she understands the difference in their skin. The poison dart frogs have smooth, shiny skin while the toad looks rough and bumpy. Talk about what smooth feels like and what bumpy feels like.

3. Give her the toad coloring page and let her color it.

4. Have her make dots of glue all over the toad, and let her pinch small portions of rice and sprinkle it over the glue. Shake off the excess.

5. When it dries, she'll have a bumpy toad to feel.

6. Make sure your child knows *T* stands for *toad*. Have her make the "t" sound.

7. Give her a crayon and let her practice writing letter *T*s on the paper.

Activity 8: Leaf-Cutting Ants

Skills learned: Letter recognition and phonics (*L* and *A*), fine motor

Materials: White, brown, and green construction paper; children's safety scissors; glue; pencil or crayon

Instructions:

1. Trace two medium-sized leaves on the green construction paper.

2. Cut an anthill shape out of the brown construction paper.

3. Explain to your child that leaf-cutting ants are found in the rain forest. They are extremely strong and carry large pieces of leaves back to their nest.

4. Let your child glue the anthill onto the white construction paper.

5. Supervise your child as she uses safety scissors to cut out the leaves.

6. Have your child pretend to be a leaf-cutting ant and tear the leaves into small pieces.

7. Let your child glue the leaf pieces to the anthill.

8. Write "LEAF-CUTTING ANTS" across the top of the project. Make sure your child knows that L stands for *leaf* and A stand for *ant*. Have her sound out the letters A and L.

9. Draw two writing practice lines on the construction paper. Put a sample L on one line and a sample A on the other line.

10. Have your child practice writing Ls and As on the handwriting practice lines.

Activity 9: Hidden *R*s

Skills learned: Letter recognition and phonics (*R*), prewriting
Materials: Paper (any kind), pencil or crayon
Instructions:

1. At the top of the paper, write an uppercase *R* and lowercase *r* and underline them. Randomly write uppercase and lowercase *R*s all over the page. Also write uppercase and lowercase *N*s, *P*s, and *B*s.

2. Explain to your child that *R* stands for *rain forest*. Make sure she can recognize uppercase and lowercase *R*s.

3. Instruct your child to find all the *R*s on the page and circle them. If she gets confused, direct her to the top of the page for a reminder of what the letter *R* looks like.

Activity 10: Bromeliad

Skills learned: Knowledge of bromeliads, fine motor

Materials: 2 paper-towel tubes, green and blue paint, paintbrush, marker

Instructions:

1. Explain to your child that a bromeliad is a plant found in the rain forest. It's known for its wide leaves that catch rainwater.

2. On one end of each tube, make three cuts at equal distances apart. The cuts should reach the middle of the tube.

3. Let your child use the marker to curl the cuts on the tube away from the center. These will be the bromeliad leaves.

4. Have your child paint the uncut parts of both tubes green.

5. When the tubes have dried, slide the uncut end of one paper-towel tube into the cut end of the other paper-towel tube. (You may have to squish the paper-towel tube that is going in to get it to fit.) Once in place, there should be two layers of bromeliad leaves.

6. Have your child use blue paint to make water drops on the leaves.

Review Time

- Can you describe what snake scales feel like?
- What does *camouflage* mean?
- What do leaf-cutting ants bring back to their anthill?
- What is the name of the rain forest plant that catches water?
- Can you find the letters *A*, *L*, *R*, and *T* in our crafts?
- What sound does *T* as in *toad* make?
- What was your favorite part of the lesson? Mine was . . .

Lesson 9

A B C D E F G H I J K L M N O P Q R S T U V W X Y Z

Apples

Featured Letters: A, S, and T

Introductory Activity: Johnny Appleseed Book

Skills learned: Familiarity with apples, fall, planting trees, pre-reading, reading comprehension, listening

Instructions:

1. Read aloud a book about Johnny Appleseed, and ask your child some comprehension questions.

2. Take this time to discuss when apples grow (fall) and the different colors and flavors of apples. Conduct a taste test, and talk about how some apples are sweet and some are sour.

Activity 2: Counting Apple Seeds

Skills learned: Counting, matching, number recognition

Materials: 5 apples cut from felt or construction paper, felt pen, felt board

Instructions:

1. Cut a felt or construction-paper apple in half lengthwise.

2. Write the number 5 on one side, and draw five seeds on the other. Repeat this for each apple, choosing numbers that will be challenging but not frustrating.

3. Put the apple halves with the numbers on one side of the felt board and the apple halves with the seeds on the other.

4. Ask your child to match the numbered halves to the appropriate seeds.

5. Then reverse the order, and let her count the seeds and find the matching number.

Activity 3: Apple Stars

Skills learned: Fine motor, letter recognition and phonics (*A* and *S*), listening

Materials: White construction paper, 1 apple, red or green paint, felt pen

Instructions:

1. In large capital letters, write "APPLE STARS" on the construction paper.

2. When an apple is cut across the middle perpendicular to the core (not lengthwise), a star is revealed.

3. Read the story that follows these instructions. At the end of the story, cut the apple across the middle to reveal the star shape of the apple core.

4. Without disturbing the shape of the star, trim the sides of the apple so it can be held easily by your child.

5. Instruct your child to dip the star of the apple in the paint and stamp it onto the lines of the words APPLE STARS.

6. Give her slices of apple to stamp apple decorations on the rest of the paper.

7. Emphasize the letter *A* stands for *apple* and *S* stands for *star*. Have her make the sounds with you.

Apple Stars

Once upon a time, there was a bunny rabbit named Sully. Sully spent most of his days hopping from garden to garden looking for food. He nibbled on lettuce and crunched on carrots, and he thought green beans and cabbage were particularly tasty. The gardens that Sully visited were perfect for a bunny rabbit, but his favorite place in the world to visit was Apple Hill. There he could find rows and rows of the most delicious apples in all the land. There were bright red apples, green apples, and yellow apples. They were sweet and juicy, and the orchard floor was always covered with apples for Sully to munch on.

One sunny afternoon, Sully was sitting in the shade under an apple tree enjoying an apple he found on the ground. He crunched on the apple and slurped up the juice when he was startled by an owl up in the tree. The owl said, "Excuse me, little bunny, but that crunching and slurping is keeping me awake." Sully replied, "It's a lovely day, Mr. Owl. Why don't you come and join me under this tree for an apple?" The owl said, "Thank you for the invitation, but I must sleep during the day so I can stay awake at night." Sully thought about that for a moment and then asked the owl, "Why would you want to stay awake at night?" The owl replied, "Well, there is plenty to see and do at night. My favorite thing is to sit high up in the tree and look up at the night sky. The stars are so beautiful." Sully thought looking at the stars sounded like so much fun, and he decided to stay awake that night to see the stars.

Sunset arrived, and Sully sat on top of a tall hill awaiting the arrival of the stars. As day turned to dusk, Sully found himself feeling very sleepy. He had been hopping from garden to garden all morning and munching on apples all afternoon. He thought he could get comfortable in the grass, see the stars, and then fall asleep. Unfortunately, Sully fell fast asleep before the stars came out.

The next morning Sully was very disappointed that he had missed seeing the stars. He went and found the owl again and told him the sad news. In an effort to cheer up his new friend, the owl said, "Did you know that you can see stars during the day as well?" Sully was confused. He said, "I'm awake every day and I have never seen a star during the day." The owl smiled and said, "You just have to know where to look. Every day you snack on apples, and you eat around the apple core. You don't realize that there is something very special in the core of the apple." At that moment, the owl fluttered his wings, causing an apple to fall from the tree. The apple landed on a rock and split open. There, sitting on the ground for Sully to see, was the core of the apple and it was in the shape of a star.

Sully was so glad to have a new friend, and he was happy to learn where he could find stars during the day. The two friends shared the apple, and that night the owl helped Sully stay awake long enough to see the stars in the sky.

Activity 4: Apple Tree

Skills learned: Counting, fine motor, letter recognition and phonics (*A* and *T*), writing

Materials: White construction paper, brown crayon or pencil, green paint, red paint, unused pencil eraser

Instructions:

1. Using the brown crayon or pencil, draw a tall tree trunk on the construction paper.

2. Have your child dip her thumb in the green paint and stamp her thumb at the top of the tree trunk to make leaves.

3. Ask your child to choose a number (either a number you have been working on or something that will be challenging, but not frustrating). This will be the number of apples she puts on the tree.

4. Tell your child that she should dip the eraser in the red paint and stamp apples on the tree. Make sure she counts as she goes and reaches the agreed-upon number of apples.

5. Write on the construction paper the letter *A* for *apple*, *T* for *tree*, and the number of apples. Sound out the letters *A* and *T*, and have your child do the same.

6. Have your child practice writing *A*s and *T*s on handwriting practice lines.

Activity 5: Torn Apple

Skills learned: Fine motor, colors

Materials: Scissors, card stock (any color), construction paper (red and green), glue

Instructions:

1. Cut out the shape of an apple from the card stock.

2. Give the red construction paper to your child, and have her tear it into pieces.

3. Let your child glue the pieces onto the apple shape.

4. Help her tear a piece of green construction paper for the stem and another for a leaf, and let her glue them onto the apple shape.

Activity 6: Apple Toss

Skills learned: Large motor, hand–eye coordination, counting
Materials: Basket or bucket, beanbags (or toddler socks filled with rice and tied off with string), masking tape
Instructions:
1. Pretend the beanbags are apples. Your child will toss them into the basket from a marked spot. (Use masking tape to mark the spot.)
2. Have her count how many times she makes it in the basket.

Activity 7: Apple Bowl Comparison

Skills learned: Comparing same and different, more and less; counting; number recognition; colors; matching
Materials: Construction paper, color pencils or crayons
Instructions:
1. Draw four bowls on the construction paper with the color pencils. Use three different colors so two bowls are the same color—for example, one blue bowl, one red bowl, and two green bowls. Make sure two bowls are the same size. For example, draw a large bowl, a medium bowl, and two small bowls of equal size. Draw apples in each bowl. Make sure each bowl has a different number of apples.
2. Have your child count the number of apples in each bowl.
3. Write the number of apples onto each bowl after your child counts them.
4. Ask your child to identify the bowls with matching colors.
5. Ask your child to identify the bowl that is the biggest, the smallest, and the two that match in size.
6. Point to two bowls, and ask your child which one has more apples.

7. Point to two more bowls, and ask which bowl has fewer apples.

8. Ask your child to identify specific numbers written on the bowls. For example, if there is a bowl with the number 9, ask her to point to it.

9. Ask your child if the bowls are the same or different. What makes them different?

Activity 8: Apple Hide-and-Seek

Skills learned: Large motor, logic
Materials: 1 apple
Instructions:

1. Have your child cover her eyes while you hide an apple somewhere in the room. Sometimes hiding it in plain sight is a good idea for beginners.

2. Let her seek for the apple. If she needs help locating the apple, tell her she's getting "hot" if she's close or "cold" if she's looking in the wrong place.

3. After she's found it, let her hide it for you. Tell her she can use the words *hot* and *cold* to help you, too.

Activity 9: Apple Puzzle

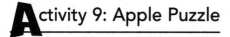

Skills learned: Logic, fine motor, hand–eye coordination
Materials: Construction paper, scissors
Instructions:

1. Cut a large apple out of construction paper, and cut the apple into three or four pieces.

2. Let your child put the puzzle back together.

Activity 10: Apple Guessing

Skills learned: Logic, discrimination, counting, colors

Materials: White construction or printer paper, color pencils or crayons

Instructions:

1. Draw four apples on the white paper with the color pencils or crayons. Make one apple red with one leaf, one red with two leaves, one green with one leaf, and one yellow with no leaves.

2. Place the paper with the four apples in front of your child. You will give her a series of hints as to which apple you want her to identify. For example, tell her the apple you want her to find is not yellow, has one leaf, and is red. Or tell her the apple you want her to find has one leaf and is not red.

3. After she has identified the apples, let her give you hints to guess which apple she wants you to find.

Review Time

- What shape can be found in the core of an apple?
- What does an apple taste like? What colors can apples be?
- Can you find the letters *A* and *T* in our crafts?
- What sounds do *A* as in *apple* and *T* as in *tree* make?
- What was your favorite part of the lesson? Mine was . . .

Lesson 10

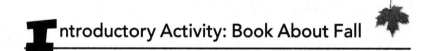

Fall

Featured Letters: F, L, and T

Introductory Activity: Book About Fall

Skills learned: Prereading, knowledge of fall, reading comprehension, listening

Instructions:

1. Read aloud a book about fall, and ask your child some comprehension questions.

2. Take this time to discuss the different seasons and what makes fall special. You may want to talk about how the weather changes, what happens to the trees, the clothes you may wear, and the holidays that occur.

Activity 2: Painted-Leaves Door Decoration

Skills learned: Fine motor, letter recognition and phonics (*F*)

Materials: 2 pieces of white constructions paper, scissors, paint in fall colors (brown, yellow, orange, red), medicine droppers, small sponge, hole punch, yarn, black marker

Instructions:

1. Cut large leaves from the white construction paper.

2. Let your child use the medicine droppers to drop paint onto the leaf cutouts.

3. Help her fold the leaves in half.

4. Have her rub the leaves and open them up to see the fall colors mixed together on each leaf.

5. In large capital letters, write "FALL" across the top of the second piece of construction paper.

6. Have your child sound out the word *fall*.

7. Give your child a small sponge, and let her sponge paint the letters on the word *fall*, using the fall colors.

8. After everything dries, have your child glue the leaves to the construction paper.

9. Punch two holes in the construction paper, one in the upper left corner and one in the upper right corner.

10. Have your child string the yarn through the holes.

11. Tie off the string, and hang your child's new fall decoration from your front door.

Activity 3: Fall Sorting

Skills learned: Counting, sorting, fine motor

Materials: 1 egg carton, 12 acorns, 12 maple seeds, 12 pinecones, 12 small leaves, 1 container or bowl

Instructions:

1. Put the acorns, seeds, pinecones, and leaves in the container or bowl.

2. Give the bowl to your child, and have her sort the contents.

3. After the items are sorted into piles, have your child place the contents of each pile in an egg carton (each item should be placed in its own egg holder), counting as she goes.

ctivity 4: Leaf Sun-Catcher

Skills learned: Fine motor, prewriting

Materials: Two 5-by-5-inch (13 by 13 cm) pieces of clear adhesive paper, tissue paper (fall colors), water, scissors, leaf cutout or leaf cookie cutter

Instructions:

1. Let your child tear the tissue paper into small pieces to place on the sticky side of one sheet of clear adhesive paper. Have her do this until the adhesive paper is filled with tissue paper.

2. Let her sprinkle the tissue paper with water so the colors of the tissue paper blend together. Let it dry.

3. Help your child place the other piece of clear adhesive paper on top of the tissue paper.

4. Get a leaf cutout, and help your child trace the leaf shape onto the adhesive paper.

5. Cut the leaf out, and tape it to a window that gets sunlight.

Activity 5: Fall Feely Box

Skills learned: Sense of touch, imagination, memory

Materials: Shoe box, fall items (leaf, acorn, pinecone, pine needle, nuts)

Instructions:

1. Place all the fall items in the shoe box.

2. Have your child reach into the box without looking and feel around for an item.

3. Once she has an item in her hand, have her tell you what she thinks it is. Before she guesses, she should tell you what the item feels like. Is it smooth, heavy, or small?

4. After she's guessed all the items and you have discussed what each item is, then put everything back in the box. Do the exercise again, but ask her to feel around for specific items. Before she puts her hand in, have her tell you what the item should feel like.

Activity 6: Leaf Rubbings

Skills learned: Fine motor, sequencing, comparing large and small, letter recognition and phonics (*L, F*), counting, writing

Materials: Leaves of different sizes, thin construction paper, crayon

Instructions:

1. Go outside with your child and collect leaves of different sizes.

2. Take this time outside to discuss that during the fall, the leaves on the trees turn different colors and fall from the trees.

3. Bring the leaves inside, and have your child sequence them from largest to smallest.

4. Place the construction paper over the leaves, and have your child rub the side of the crayon on the construction paper.

5. Use the crayon to write the letters *F* and *L* on the construction paper. Explain that *F* stands for *fall* and *L* stands for *leaves*. Have her sound out the letters with you.

6. Have your child count the number of leaves on the construction paper and write that number on the construction paper.

7. Let your child practice writing *F*s and *L*s on the construction paper or on a separate handwriting practice sheet.

Activity 7: Leaf Prints

Skills learned: Fine and large motor, comparing size, colors
Materials: Leaves, fall-colored paints, sponge, aluminum foil or newspaper, construction paper, color pencils
Instructions:
1. Let your child sponge paint the leaves with the fall-colored paint.
2. Have her place each leaf, painted side down, on the construction paper.
3. Put the aluminum foil or newspaper over the leaves, and let your child press down on the paper with her hands.
4. Allow the paint to dry; then remove the foil or paper and leaves to uncover some beautiful leaf prints.
5. Give the color pencils to your child, and have her circle all the small leaves in orange, medium leaves in blue, and large leaves in yellow (or whatever colors you choose).

Activity 8: Autumn Leaves Song

Skills learned: Memory, rhythm, imagination, large motor
Instructions:
1. As you sing the song that follows these instructions, have your child act out each verse with you.
2. Before you sing, get her imagination going by telling her to pretend that you are in a yard full of leaves.
3. Ask her some questions about the leaves she imagines: What color are your leaves? How big are your leaves? Do your leaves make a crunching noise when you walk on them?
4. Encourage your child to sing with you.

Autumn Leaves Are Falling Down (to the tune of "London Bridge Is Falling Down")

Autumn leaves are falling down, (Flutter your fingers down to
   the ground.)

Falling down, falling down.

Autumn leaves are falling down,

To the ground.

Use a rake to make a pile, (Pretend to rake the leaves.)

Make a pile, make a pile.

Use a rake to make a pile,

Now have some fun.

Jump in the pile, and throw some leaves, (Jump in the imaginary
   pile and throw up the leaves.)

Throw some leaves, throw some leaves.

Jump in the pile and throw some leaves,

In the air.

Use a rake to make a pile, (Rake the leaves again.)

Make a pile, make a pile.

Use a rake to make a pile,

Now bag it up. (Hold out an imaginary bag for your child to fill
   with leaves.)

Activity 9: Crumbled-Leaf Art

Skills learned: Fine motor, prewriting

Materials: Leaves, construction paper, glue, cotton–tip applicator,
crayon, leaf cutout

Instructions:

1. Collect fall leaves with your child.

2. Let your child trace the leaf onto the construction paper several
times.

3. Give her the glue and have her use a cotton-tip applicator to cover each leaf on the construction paper with glue.

4. Instruct your child to crumble the leaves you gathered outside and sprinkle the pieces onto the glue.

Activity 10: Fall Tree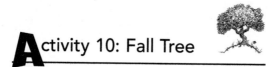

Skills learned: Letter recognition and phonics (*T*), prewriting, fine motor

Materials: Pencil with eraser, construction paper, fall-colored paints, paintbrush

Instructions:

1. Draw the outline of a tree trunk on the construction paper.

2. Have your child use the paintbrush to paint the tree trunk brown.

3. Give the remaining paints and the pencil to your child, and let her dip the eraser in the paint and stamp leaves onto the tree.

4. Write the word TREE at the top of the paper.

5. Sound out the word with your child, making sure she knows *T* stands for *tree*.

6. Let your child practice writing *T*s on the construction paper around her tree.

Variation:

For a more challenging activity, instruct your child to stamp a specific number of colored leaves. Make sure you choose numbers you are currently working on with your child. For example, stamp 12 red leaves, 9 yellow leaves, and 15 orange leaves.

Activity 11: Autumn Words

Skills learned: Writing, phonics

Materials: Printer paper, pencil or crayon

Instructions:

1. Write or print fall words (e.g., LEAF, FALL, TREE, PINECONE) on the printer paper, omitting the first letter of each word. For example, write "__ EAF" for LEAF. It would also be helpful, but not necessary, to draw each of the items next to its word.

2. Give the pencil or crayon to your child.

3. Tell her each word, and have her sound out the beginning sound and tell you what letter it is.

4. Have her write the missing letter in the blank. (Give her a helping hand if she's not writing yet.)

Activity 12: Catch the Falling Leaf

Skills learned: Large motor, hand-eye coordination
Materials: Construction paper (any fall color), black marker, children's safety scissors, beanbag
Instructions:

1. Use the marker to draw a large leaf on the construction paper.

2. Let your child cut out the leaf using children's safety scissors. If she's not quite ready to cut, do the cutting for her.

3. Use the beanbag to toss the leaf in the air. Do this by placing the leaf on top of the beanbag and then tossing the beanbag until it hits the ceiling. Catch the beanbag as it comes down, and let your child catch the falling leaf.

4. Do this activity in an open space. Your child's eyes will be focused on catching the leaf and not on where she is walking, so make sure there are no obstructions in her way.

Review Time

- What colors do leaves change to in the fall?
- What happens to the leaves after they change color?
- Can you find the letters *F*, *L*, and *T* in our crafts?
- What sounds do *F* as in *fall*, *L* as in *leaf*, and *T* as in *tree*, make?
- What numbers did we talk about in our activities?
- What was your favorite part of the lesson? Mine was . . .

Lesson 11

Shapes

Featured Letters: D, H, O, R, S, and T

Introductory Activity: Book About Shapes

Skills learned: Prereading, knowledge of shapes, reading comprehension, listening

Instructions:

1. Read aloud a book about shapes, and ask your child some comprehension questions.

2. Take this time to discuss shapes.

3. Ask your child to list as many shapes as he can think of.

4. Encourage your child to talk about what makes shapes different from one another.

Activity 2: Mystery Shapes Felt Board

Skills learned: Shapes, color recognition, listening, rhyming, counting

Materials: Felt board (optional); felt, fabric interfacing, or construction paper (different colors); scissors

Instructions:

1. Cut out the following shapes from felt or construction paper of different colors: circle, square, diamond, rectangle, triangle, oval, and heart. If you are using fabric interfacing, color each shape a different color.

2. Let your child look at all the shapes, and help him become familiar with them.

3. Let your child hold the shapes while you read the poem that follows these instructions.

4. Ask your child to help you figure out what shape you are describing.

5. Invite your child to put the shapes on the felt board as you mention them during the poem. Emphasize the color of each shape.

6. Also emphasize which shapes have straight lines and which have curves. Help him count the number of sides.

7. While your child is still learning his shapes, you may want to hold up the shape you are describing and ask him to name it.

Shapes Mystery

I have four sides, but I am not a square.
I'm a kite without a tail that floats up in the air.
Which shape am I? (*diamond*)

My sides are not straight, but curved like a ball.
Unlike my cousin, oval, I'm not very tall.
Which shape am I? (*circle*)

I look like a box. Do you know my name?
I have four equal sides, and their lengths are the same!
Which shape am I? (*square*)

I am a unique shape, the symbol of love.
On Valentine's Day I am what you think of.
What shape am I? (*heart*)

I have four straight lines; two long ones are equal size.
The other two are shorter. Can you guess this surprise?
Which shape am I? (*rectangle*)

I have one curvy line, but I'm not round like a pie.
I'm a little bit longer, like the shape of your eye.
Which shape am I? (*oval*)

I also have lines that are straight on me,
But I don't have four sides—I only have three!
Which shape am I? (*triangle*)

Activity 3: Match-the-Shapes Place Mat

Skills learned: Shapes, fine motor, color recognition, counting
Materials: 8 pieces of construction paper (different colors), scissors, children's safety scissors, black marker, glue
Instructions:
1. Choose one piece of construction paper to use as the place mat and set it aside.
2. Use the remaining pieces of construction paper to cut out the following shapes: oval, square, diamond, heart, rectangle, circle, and triangle. Or make outlines of each shape, and supervise your child as he uses safety scissors to cut out the shapes.
3. Have your child trace the shapes on the piece of construction paper set aside for the place mat. Look at the place mat with your child and familiarize him with each shape.
4. Give the shapes to your child, and help him match each shape to the shape on the place mat. Repeat this process a couple times.

5. Let your child glue each shape on the matching outline.

6. Help your child count the number of sides on each shape and the number of shapes on the place mat.

7. Laminate the finished product so the place mat can be used again.

Activity 4: *T* Is for Triangle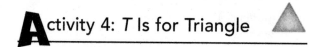

Skills learned: Letter recognition and phonics (*T*), writing, fine motor, shapes

Materials: Pencil or crayon, children's safety scissors, construction paper

Instructions:

1. Trace a large triangle on the construction paper.

2. Supervise as your child cuts out the triangle with safety scissors.

3. Make sure your child knows *T* stands for *triangle*. Sound it out together.

4. Draw a handwriting practice line on the triangle and a sample *T*.

5. Give the pencil or crayon to your child, and let him practice writing *T*s on the handwriting practice line.

Activity 5: Tissue-Paper Place Mat

Skills learned: Shapes, fine motor, color recognition

Materials: 8 pieces of tissue paper (different colors), 1 piece of white construction paper, white vinegar, paintbrush

Instructions:

1. Using all the different pieces of tissue paper, cut out the following shapes: oval, square, diamond, heart, rectangle, circle, triangle, and star.

2. Give the shapes to your child, and have him tell you the name of each shape.

3. Place the shapes on a piece of white construction paper, and let your child brush vinegar onto each shape with a paintbrush. A little vinegar goes a long way!

4. After the vinegar dries, the tissue paper will fall off, leaving a stain of each shape.

5. Take the finished product to a copy center for lamination or use clear contact paper or a laminating kit found at craft stores so the place mat can be used over and over.

Activity 6: I Spy Shapes

Skills learned: Listening, shapes
Instructions:

1. Take your child around your home. Say, "I spy a rectangle," and help your child find as many rectangles as he can. Repeat this with different shapes.

2. Let your child say, "I spy a . . ." for you to guess.

Activity 7: Cardboard Shapes

Skills learned: Fine motor, shapes, placement vocabulary, prewriting
Materials: Cardboard, crayon, paper, scissors
Instructions:

1. Cut out several different shapes from a piece of cardboard.

2. Place the cardboard shapes over the paper for your child to trace.

3. Let your child use a crayon to trace each shape onto the paper.

4. After the shapes are traced, show your child how to draw lines inside of the shapes. Show him how to draw from left to right, up and down, and diagonally.

5. Ask him to give it a try, and give him a helping hand if needed.

Activity 8: Letter and Shape Match

Skills learned: Letter recognition and phonics (*D, H, O, R, S,* and *T*), shapes, fine motor, colors recognition

Materials: Construction paper (various colors), pencil or crayon, children's safety scissors

Instructions:

1. On a sheet of construction paper, write in large print the letters *T, R, S, D, O,* and *H.*

2. Trace a triangle, rectangle, square, diamond, octagon, and hexagon on construction paper, using a different color for each shape, and make the shapes large enough to cover the letters you wrote.

3. Supervise as your child uses safety scissors to cut out the various shapes.

4. Discuss with your child each shape and its color.

5. Sound out the name of the shape, and ask your child to identify what letter the name begins with.

6. Glue the top portion of the shape over the letter so that later your child can look at the shape, identify the beginning letter, and flip the shape up to check if he is correct.

Activity 9: Photo Album Shapes

Skills learned: Fine motor, shapes, counting, prewriting

Materials: Construction paper, small photo album with pages that peel back, dry-erase marker, scissors

Instructions:

1. Cut out several shapes from the construction paper.

2. Put each shape on its own page in a small photo album. The album should have peeling, sticky pages so the shapes stay in place.

3. Have your child use a dry-erase marker to trace the shape onto the pages of the album. Help him recognize each shape, its color, and its number of sides.

4. Use a paper towel to wipe away the markings so he can use the book again.

Activity 10: Simon Says

Skills learned: Listening, large motor, shapes, placement vocabulary, counting

Materials: Masking tape

Instructions:

1. Use the masking tape to make several large shapes on the floor.

2. Play Simon Says with your child.

Simon says:

Jump over the circle.

Hop on one foot on the oval.

Balance on a corner of the triangle on one foot.

Walk around the square.

Count the sides of the rectangle.

Walk forward to the star.

Walk backward to the diamond.

Activity 11: Magazine Cutouts

Skills learned: Fine motor, shapes, sorting

Materials: 1 children's magazine, children's safety scissors, construction paper

Instructions:

1. Cut different large shapes out of the construction paper.

2. Let your child look through a magazine for different shapes. (Make sure it's a children's magazine so he doesn't come across any inappropriate ads.)

3. Supervise while your child cuts out the shapes he finds.

4. Have your child first sort all the shapes, then glue each onto its matching cutout—for example, all the squares onto a square cutout.

Activity 12: Shapes Feely Box

Skills learned: Memory, shapes, sorting, fine motor
Materials: Cardboard, shoe box
Instructions:

1. Cut out different shapes, such as stars, circles, ovals, triangles, and squares, from the cardboard. Cut two or three of each shape, and put them in the shoe box.

2. Invite your child to put his hand in the shoe box without looking, and have him identify the shape he grabs.

3. When the shoe box is empty, play again. This time ask him to find all of the ovals, all of the stars, and so on.

Activity 13: Find the Shapes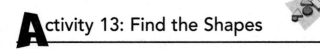

Skills learned: Shapes, fine motor, prewriting
Materials: Construction paper, black marker, crayons
Instructions:

1. Draw circles, squares, and triangles on the construction paper.

2. Have your child color all the circles, mark an X over all the squares, and circle all the triangles.

Variation:

For a greater challenge, follow the preceding instructions but include ovals and rectangles on the construction paper. This way, your child will have to differentiate between ovals and circles, and between squares and rectangles.

Review Time

- What is your favorite shape? Why?
- How many sides does a triangle have? A rectangle? A diamond?
- Does a circle have a curvy or straight line?
- Can you find the letters *D, R, S,* and *T* in our crafts?
- What sound does *R* as in *rectangle* make?
- What was your favorite part of the lesson? Mine was . . .

Lesson 12

A B C D E F G H I J K L M N O P Q R S T U V W X Y Z

Forest

Featured Letter: A

Introductory Activity: Forest Animal Book

Skills learned: Listening, prereading, knowledge of forest life, reading comprehension

Instructions:

1. Read aloud a picture book about the forest with your child. Try to find one about the forest in the winter; otherwise, any forest book will do. You may also want to find a book showing paw prints of the animals that live in the forest. Ask your child comprehension questions about the story you read.

2. Discuss how a forest is different from other habitats, who lives in the forest, and what vegetation you can find there.

Activity 2: Animal Riddles

Skills learned: Logic, listening, knowledge of animals

Materials: Animal riddles, pictures of animals (drawn, printed from a computer, or book illustrations)

Instructions:

1. Have your child brainstorm the different animals that live in the forest.

2. Ask your child riddles. You may need to prompt your child with extra clues to elicit an answer. Here are some examples:

> I am black and white with a striped tail and I wear a mask. I only come out at night. (*raccoon*)
>
> I walk around on my four long legs. I have hooves. If I'm a boy, I grow antlers. I can jump over fences with ease. (*deer*)
>
> I live in the trees. I eat acorns and nuts. I have a long bushy tail. (*squirrel*)
>
> I live in trees. I fly out at night to hunt. I like to eat mice and small rodents. I sleep during the day. I say "whoo." (*owl*)
>
> I am large and hairy. I eat meat and vegetables. I hibernate during the winter. I like to growl. (*bear*)

3. Show your child the picture of the animal when he gets the answer correct.

Variation:

If you need to make this activity easier, have several animal pictures displayed and let your child point out the correct animal.

ctivity 3: Bear Cookies

Skills learned: Fine motor, following directions, discrimination by size, shapes

Materials: Chilled, plain and chocolate sugar-cookie dough; wax paper; refrigerator; plastic wrap; safe plastic knives; oven; chocolate chips; light-brown candy-coated chocolates

Instructions:

1. Soften up the chilled cookie dough so that your child can manipulate it.

2. Clean your child's hands, and help her roll the chocolate dough into one thick log and one thinner log. Roll the plain dough into one very thin log.

3. Wrap the logs with plastic wrap, and chill for at least an hour.

4. Preheat the oven to the temperature required for your dough.

5. Cut each dough log into ⅜-inch (1 cm) slices.

6. Have your child get a large chocolate slice to make the bear face, two smaller chocolate slices to make the ears, and one plain slice to be the muzzle. Then let her add a chocolate chip nose and candy-coated chocolate eyes.

7. Bake the cookies according to the recipe or product directions. *Note:* This is a good time to remind your child to be careful around the oven and hot cookie sheets.

Activity 4: Felt-Board Animals

Skills learned: Logic, concept of difference, visual discrimination, left and right

Materials: Construction paper or card stock, felt board, masking tape, glue, scissors

Instructions:

1. Make animal pictures in sets of three by drawing them on your cardstock or construction paper or by using clip art or color pages from the Internet. The pictures in each set should be identical except for one picture in which you alter *one* feature. You may reverse the direction it faces, change the color, remove a body part, or make some other alteration. Put masking tape on the back of the pictures.

2. Display the animal sets on the felt board, and ask your child to identify which one is different in each set and why.

Activity 5: Raccoon Touch

Skills learned: Logic, sense of touch, fine motor

Materials: Large empty tissue box or a shoe box with a hole cut in the top of it, different objects with definite shape and texture

Instructions:

1. Place the objects in the mystery box. Decorate the mystery box if you choose.

2. Discuss raccoons with your child, and talk about their inherent curiosity.

3. Have your child pretend to be a raccoon and reach into the mystery box to find objects that you ask for. For example: tell her to feel around and pull out a toy car.

Variation:

To make this activity easier, you can show your child the objects before putting them into the box. Ask her to find them.

Activity 6: Up a Tree

Skills learned: Large motor, letter and number recognition, phonics, dramatic play

Materials: Masking tape, large floor area, construction-paper leaves

Instructions:

1. Tape the outline of a tree and branches onto your floor. Write different numbers and letters on the paper leaves, and tape them to the tree.

2. Tell your child that today she is going to pretend to be a squirrel. Discuss how squirrels climb trees by jumping from branch to branch.

3. Ask your child to start at the bottom of the tree. Then direct her to jump to the leaves, based on their letter or number. For example: tell her to jump to the leaf with the letter *A*, the leaf with a number 9, or the leaf with the letter that says "b."

Activity 7: Squirrel Math

Skills learned: Logic, fine motor, listening, addition, subtraction, counting, math vocabulary, rhyming

Materials: Large pile of real or paper acorns

Instructions:

1. Discuss with your child that in the fall squirrels collect nuts and acorns to store up for winter. Then tell her that she is going to hear a poem about one such squirrel and solve some math problems.

2. Give your child the pile of acorns, and tell her that she is going to learn how to add and subtract. As you read the poem, prompt her with the meanings of *add*, *subtract*, *equal*, and *sum*.

3. Read aloud the following poem. Help your child solve the problem by manipulating the acorns. Continue to work on new problems by changing the amount of acorns. Do not let your child get too frustrated. Assist her as much as necessary.

> *Squirrel Math*
> I saw a little squirrel. He was as busy as could be.
> He was hoarding lots of acorns in his evergreen tree.
> First he found three (substitute other numbers) acorns, and then
>   he found one.
> How many did that *equal*? Can you figure out the *sum*?

Or,

First he found four (substitute other numbers) acorns, and then
   he found two.

How many did that *equal*? I can *add* it up, can you?

Then,

As winter winds began to howl, and food was hard to find,

Squirrel said, "I'll nest in my tree, if you don't mind."

He climbed in and snuggled down to take a winter's sleep,

Until his belly's rumble said, "Wake up! It's time to eat."

He opened up his acorn hoard and found a pile of ten.

If three acorns (substitute other numbers) were gobbled up, what
   was *left* then?

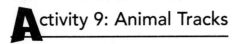ctivity 8: A Is for *Acorn*

Skills learned: Fine motor, letter recognition and phonics (*A*), writing

Materials: Light-brown construction paper, crayon, children's safety
scissors

Instructions:

1. Draw a simple, large acorn on the construction paper. Draw a
handwriting practice line across the center of the acorn, and write a
sample *A* at the beginning of the line.

2. Give your child the acorn picture and crayon. Help her practice
writing her *A*s on the handwriting practice line; then have her cut
the acorn out.

Activity 9: Animal Tracks

Skills learned: Knowledge of animal tracks, fine motor, prewriting

Materials: Large manila paper, black pen or marker, crayon

Instructions:

1. Draw or print from clip art or the Internet small pictures of different forest animals: raccoon, bear, or squirrel. Cut these out.

2. From the Internet or your local library, obtain a sample of each animal's track. To start, pick one animal and draw its tracks across the construction paper. Choose the next animal and draw its tracks across the paper in a different direction, making sure to intersect with the first set of tracks in at least one spot. Continue with all of the animal tracks to create a wandering jumble of tracks on the paper.

3. Give your child the page of tracks. Show her the cutout picture of the bear, and point to one example of a bear track. Have her find where the bear tracks begin on the paper. Then have her follow the bear tracks on the paper with a crayon, connecting the tracks as she goes. This is much like a dot-to-dot. Have her glue the picture of the bear at the end of the trail. Then repeat with each of the other animals.

Activity 10: The Squirrel Runs into the Hole

Skills learned: Large motor

Materials: Shoe box with lid, masking tape, small ball or large marble, milk- or juice-carton lids

Instructions:

1. Remove the box lid, and turn the lid upside down. Place it on top of the shoe box, and tape *one* edge of the lid to the edge of the shoe box. Cut a hole slightly larger than your ball in the center of the lid. Glue several carton lids into the shoe-box lid to act as barriers. This is your squirrel game.

2. Give your child the squirrel game, and place the ball in the shoe-box lid. Tell her that the ball is a squirrel, and she must help the squirrel run into the hole to hide.

3. Have her wiggle the box around until her squirrel falls into the hole.

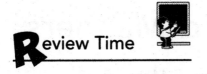

Review Time

- Can you find the letter *A* in our crafts?
- What do squirrels like to eat?
- What is a track?
- What was your favorite activity in this lesson? Mine was . . .

Lesson 13

A B C D E F G H I J K L M N O P Q R S T U V W X Y Z

Feelings and Manners

Featured Letters: F, M, and P

Introductory Activity: Book About Manners

Skills learned: Prereading, knowledge of good manners, reading comprehension, listening

Instructions:

1. Read aloud a book about manners, and ask your child a few comprehension questions.

2. Take this time to discuss good manners. Ask your child what he should do when he coughs or sneezes. What should he say if somebody else sneezes? When would he say, "Please," "Thank you," or "Excuse me"?

Activity 2: Introductions, Please

Skills learned: Knowledge of introductions

Instructions:

Take turns doing introductions. Don't forget to shake hands!

- "Hello, my name is Terry."
- "Pleased to meet you, Terry, my name is Jane."
- "Pleased to meet you, too."

Activity 3: Miss Manners

Skills learned: Knowledge of good manners and bad manners, fine motor, letter recognition and phonics (*M*)

Materials: Paper plate, crayons, craft stick

Instructions:

1. Help your child make a happy face on one side of the paper plate and a sad face on the other side.

2. Glue the craft stick onto the plate so your child can hold it.

3. Write a letter *M* on the craft stick. Make sure your child knows *M* stands for *manners*, and have him sound it out.

4. Read the following scenarios (or make up some of your own), and have him hold up the plate and show you the appropriate face. (Avoid using your own child or his friends as an example of bad manners. He may get his feelings hurt, or he may even object and rightfully start an argument when he should be focusing on the exercise.)

Billy Bear asked for a glass of milk without saying, "Please."

Penny Princess covered her mouth when she sneezed.

When playgroup was over, Russ said, "Thank you," to his friend for having him over.

Billy Bear said, "Excuse me," to his friend when he needed to get past him.

Penny Princess talked to everyone at the table with food in her mouth.

Russ grabbed a toy from his friend.

Billy Bear said, "Good night," to everyone before going to bed. Penny Princess quickly said, "Sorry," to her friend for accidentally bumping into her.

Russ interrupted his mommy and daddy while they were talking. Billy Bear patiently waited his turn to go down the slide at the playground.

5. After each example reinforce the good manners or explain what the person should have done by saying, "We always say, 'Please,' when we ask for something," or "We don't grab toys from our friends. Russ should have waited until his friend was finished playing with the toy."

Activity 4: Cover Up!

Skills learned: Saying "Excuse me," fine motor
Materials: 1 paper plate, construction paper, scissors, glue, 1 tissue, black marker, pencil
Instructions:
1. Have your child help you draw his face on the paper plate. Either he can draw or he can tell you where to put the eyes, nose, and mouth.
2. Use the pencil to trace his hands on the construction paper, and cut them out.
3. Explain that when people cough or sneeze, they cover their mouths. When people are finished, they say, "Excuse me."
4. Have him glue the tissue under the nose and over the mouth, and then have him glue the hands over the tissue.

Activity 5: Manners Obstacle Course

Skills learned: Taking turns, being patient

Materials: Household items such as pillows, step stools, chairs

Instructions:

1. Set up an obstacle course in your house by using pillows for jumping over, tables for walking around, or chairs for crawling under.

2. Explain that he can go first and you will follow.

3. The next time, you go first and he follows. Make sure he understands to take turns, to not push, and to never cut in front of the line.

Variation:

1. This is also a great exercise for more than one child.

2. Have the children start on opposite sides of the course. When they come face-to-face with one another, they need to say, "Excuse me," in order to pass.

Activity 6: *P* Is for *Please*

Skills learned: Letter recognition and phonics (*P*), writing, manners

Materials: 2 pieces of construction paper, pencil or crayon, scissors, glue

Instructions:

1. Cut out a large letter *P* from one piece of construction paper.

2. Let your child glue it to the other piece of construction paper.

3. Make sure your child knows that *P* stands for *please*, and have him sound out the letter *P*.

4. Have your child tell you all the instances where he would say "please."

5. Write what your child says on the construction paper.

6. Let your child practice writing *P*s on the large letter *P*.

Activity 7: Sharing Box Activity

Skills learned: Taking turns, sharing, large and fine motor

Materials: Toys, box, kitchen timer

Instructions:

1. Fill a box with toys, and put them in the center of the room.

2. Invite your child to go choose a toy from the box, and choose one for yourself.

3. Set the kitchen timer for 2 or 3 minutes.

4. Explain that when the time is up, both of you have to put your respective toys back in the box and choose another toy.

5. Make sure he understands that people take turns when they play with toys and they share. Have fun sharing!

Activity 8: Puppet Feelings

Skills learned: Creativity, imagination, dramatic play

Materials: Small paper lunch bags, construction paper, glue

Instructions:

1. From the construction paper, cut out rectangles that are the same size as the bottom of the paper bag.

2. Ask your child to describe different emotions.

3. Draw a face with a different emotion on each rectangle: happy, sad, surprised, or any other emotion you would like to teach your child.

4. Put the faces showing emotion on the table, and let your child choose some to use on his paper bags.

5. Have him glue them onto the bottom flap of the bags.

6. Ask him what sort of things make his happy puppet so happy, or why he thinks his sad puppet is sad.

7. Put on a puppet show with him.

Activity 9: Snack Sharing

Skills learned: Use of "May I," "Please," and "Thank you"

Materials: 3–4 small plates of your child's favorite snacks

Instructions:

1. Place the plates on the table. Some of the plates should be close to you and some should be close to him.

2. If he would like a snack that is out of his reach, have him politely ask you to pass it:

"Mommy, may I have some cheese?"

"Yes, you may."

"Thank you."

"You're welcome."

3. You should also ask for snacks that are out of your reach so he can practice saying, "You're welcome."

4. Make sure he asks to be excused before leaving the table.

Activity 10: "Help Set the Table" Place Mat

Skills learned: Knowledge of how to properly make a place setting, fine motor, shapes

Materials: Construction paper (various colors), children's safety scissors, glue

Instructions:

1. On several different colors of construction paper, draw a circle the size of a plate, a smaller circle the size of a dessert plate, a circle the size of a cup, a triangle the size of a napkin, a fork, a knife, and a spoon.

2. Help your child cut out all of the paper dinnerware.

3. Let him arrange the place setting on another piece of construction paper. The fork goes on the left on top of the napkin, then the plate, then the knife with the sharp edge facing the plate, and then the spoon. The cup circle goes in the upper right part of the construction paper.

4. Have him glue the pieces in place.

5. Flip the place mat over, and let him glue the dessert plate down.

6. Now your child can help set the table by matching the dinnerware to the place mat.

7. When he has finished eating dinner, he can flip the place mat over for desert.

8. Laminate this one so it can be used again.

Activity 11: Feelings Stories

Skills learned: Imagination, letter recognition and phonics (*F*), fine motor

Materials: 2 pieces of construction paper (one white and one any color), children's safety scissors, parenting magazine, glue

Instructions:

1. Use the colored construction paper to cut out a large letter *F*.

2. Let your child glue the letter *F* onto the white construction paper. Make sure he knows how to make the "f" sound.

3. Give the magazine to your child, and let him cut out pictures of people or kids with different expressions on their faces.

4. Have your child glue his pictures onto the white construction paper.

5. Ask your child about each picture. Have him describe the expression and what may have caused the expression.

6. Write down what your child says under each picture.

Review Time

- If Mommy and Daddy are talking and you need to ask a question, what do you say? (*Excuse me*)
- Can you tell me how you would use your good manners to ask for a cup of milk? (*Please*)
- After I get you the cup of milk, what do you say? (*Thank you*)
- What are some ways you can share?
- What are different kinds of feelings?
- Can you find the letters *F*, *M*, and *P* in our activities?
- What sound does *P* as in *please* make?
- What was your favorite part of the lesson? Mine was . . .

Lesson 14

A B C D E F G H I J K L M N O P Q R S T U V W X Y Z

Winter Days

Featured Letter: I

Introductory Activity: Winter Story

Skills learned: Listening, prereading, reading comprehension, knowledge of winter

Instructions:

1. Read aloud any winter story to your child. Be sure to stop periodically to ask comprehension questions.

2. Take this time to discuss your area's winter weather conditions and activities.

Activity 2: Make a Snowflake

Skills learned: Fine motor, folding, knowledge of snow, shapes, concept of *unique*

Materials: White tissue–paper squares or circles (paper doilies work great too), construction paper, glue, children's safety scissors

Instructions:

1. Discuss snow and that no two snowflakes are alike, just as there is no one else like your child.

2. Have your child fold her tissue paper in half bringing short sides together.

3. Fold it in half the short way again; then holding the double-folded corner, fold the paper into a triangle by bringing opposite corners together.

4. Help your child cut shapes out of each side of the triangle.

5. When you unfold the paper, you should see a unique snowflake.

6. Have her make several snowflakes. Mount them on construction paper, attach a string to each snowflake and hang them up.

Activity 3: Ice and Crystal Experiments

Skills learned: Knowledge of ice, color mixing, fine motor

Materials: Water, plastic container (1–2-pint size [0.5–1 L]), liquid food coloring in dropper bottles, rock salt, baking pan

Instructions:

1. Make an ice block by freezing water inside a plastic container overnight.

2. Discuss that ice is frozen water. What happens when ice melts? The ice becomes water.

3. Place the ice block in a pan in front of your child.

4. Have her sprinkle on rock salt. This will melt the ice quickly.

5. Now put a few drops of two different food colors on top of the ice block. As the ice melts, the colors will blend. Discuss the color combinations and what the two colors become: red and yellow make orange, red and blue make purple, and blue and yellow make green. What makes brown? Black?

Activity 4: Let's Build Some Snowmen

Skills learned: Fine motor, logic, size discrimination, memory
Materials: White and colored construction paper or fabric interfacing, felt board, masking tape, crayon
Instructions:
1. Draw three snowmen on the white construction paper or interfacing in three different sizes. Be sure to draw in their faces and buttons down the front. Cut out the snowmen, and then cut off their heads.
2. From the colored construction paper, cut out hats, scarves, and boots to fit the small, medium, and large snowmen.
3. Display the snowman bodies on the felt board, and then ask your child to match the snowman heads to the different-sized bodies. Next have her match the scarves as well as each of the other items. Remember that your child should base her decision on size.
4. Take down the small and medium snowmen, and ask your child to close her eyes. Remove one item from the large snowman. Have your child open her eyes, and ask her if she can tell you what item you removed from the snowman. See if she also can remember what color the item was.

Activity 5: Snowball Math

Skills learned: Prediction, counting, fine motor
Materials: Small cotton balls, white and blue construction paper, glue
Instructions:
1. Cut out several white construction-paper circles in different sizes. These are paper snowballs. Glue them on the blue construction paper.

2. Give your child the paper with the snowballs, and show her a small cotton ball. Tell her that she is going to pretend the cotton balls are snow. She has to cover each paper snowball with snow. How many cotton balls does she think it will take to cover the first snowball? Write her prediction under the snowball. Discuss that a prediction is a guess based on what a person knows.

3. Next have her glue cotton balls to fill the snowball. Have her count the cotton balls. How many did it actually take to cover the snowball? Write that number under her prediction. Continue with the rest of the snowballs.

Activity 6: Snowman Sequence Cards

Skills learned: Sequencing
Materials: 5 index cards or paper, black marker
Instructions:
1. Draw one of the five stages of a snowman melting on each of the five index cards.
2. Mix up the cards, and have your child put them into order.
3. You could also let her pretend to be a melting snowman afterward.

Activity 7: *I* Is for *Ice*

Skills learned: Fine motor, writing, letter recognition, phonics (*I*)
Materials: White construction paper, crayon, children's safety scissors, black marker
Instructions:
1. Draw a simple large rectangle (ice cube) on the construction paper. Draw a handwriting practice line across the ice, and write a sample *I* at the beginning.

2. Give your child the ice picture, and help her practice writing her *I*s. Discuss what sound an *I* makes and that *ice* begins with *I*.

3. Have her cut out the ice cube. Draw an igloo for short "i" sound.

Activity 8: Snow Thoughts

Skills learned: Language, prereading
Materials: Printed or written sentence starters, pen
Instructions:

1. Print several statements about snow, but leave out the ending of each sentence. For example:

Snowflakes fall as quietly as _____.
The snow is as cold as _____.
Snow makes me happy because _____.
Snow sometimes makes me sad because _____.

2. Read each sentence with your child, and guide her in coming up with some descriptive words to fill in the blanks.

3. If you live in an area without snow, substitute the snow questions with winter questions such as

Winter is as cold as _____.
Winter makes me happy because _____.
Winter sometimes makes me sad because _____.

Activity 9: I Can Ice-Skate

Skills learned: Large motor, dramatic play
Materials: Wax paper, wide rubber bands, carpeted area
Instructions:

1. Make sure that the floor area you choose is free of furniture and hard objects. Wax-paper skating is very slippery! Clear out any objects your child could fall on in the area that she will be skating in, and be nearby to lend a helping hand.

2. Wrap a large wax-paper rectangle on your child's feet with the slick side out. Attach it by wrapping rubber bands around her ankles.

3. Let her pretend to ice-skate around the room by sliding her feet. Again, be certain your child is on a soft floor and the area is free of obstacles.

Activity 10: The Dress-Up Game

Skills learned: Large and fine motor, life skills

Materials: Various items of winter clothing (include snaps, zippers, and buttons), masking tape, duffle bag

Instructions:

1. Pack one winter duffle bag for each team. Items in each bag should require the same amount of time and be similar in difficulty to put on. If you are working with one child then team two will be the parent. Make your dress-up bag accordingly. Make a starting line with masking tape and move the dressing bags to the other side of the room.

2. Race to the bags, get dressed in the items in the bag, run back to the starting line, and get undressed.

3. If there are several children, then the next person in line must get dressed, run to the other line and back, and get undressed. First team done wins!

Activity 11: Spoon Race

Skills learned: Large motor, balance

Materials: Several ice cubes, large wooden or plastic spoons with a large scoop, several bowls, masking tape

Instructions:

1. Tape off start and finish lines on your floor. Place a bowl at the starting line and another at the finish line.

2. Place two to four ice cubes in the bowl at the starting line, and give your child a spoon. Tell her that she must scoop an ice cube onto her spoon at the starting line and then carry the ice cube to the finish line without touching the ice cube with her fingers or dropping it. If an ice cube drops, she must take it back to the starting line and try again. The first one to get all the ice cubes to the finish line wins!

3. Let her race you or a classmate.

Review Time

- Can you find the letter *I* in our activities?
- What is ice? Snow?
- What are some fun things we do in the wintertime?
- What sound does the letter *I* as in *ice* or in *igloo* make?
- What was your favorite part of the day? Mine was . . .

Lesson 15

A B C D E F G H I J K L M N O P Q R S T U V W X Y Z

Sound

Featured Letter: B

▌ntroductory Activity: Hearing Book

Skills learned: Knowledge of senses, listening, prereading, reading comprehension

Materials: Any book about hearing, earplugs

Instructions:

1. Read aloud a book about the sense of hearing, and discuss hearing and how this sense helps people. Ask comprehension questions about the story you read.

2. Put earplugs in your child's ears, and make a soft noise that he can't hear. Speak softly so he can't hear you. Unplug his ears and ask why not being able to hear could be a problem.

3. You can also explore the concepts of *near* and *far* by covering your child's eyes and making a noise near him and another far from him. Each time, ask him to identify where you are in the room.

Activity 2: Musical Sticks

Skills learned: Large motor, concept of loud and soft, rhythm

Materials: Musical sticks (can be cut from a dowel rod) or wooden spoons, any music

Instructions:

1. Put on your music or sing a song, and have your child drum on the floor with his sticks.

2. Instruct him to beat softly, loudly, slowly, or quickly. Encourage him to drum to the beat of the music.

Activity 3: Musical Instruments

Skills learned: Fine and large motor, creativity, sound exploration, letter recognition

Materials: Paper plates, rice or beans, stapler or glue, decorations of choice (e.g., stickers, paper, crayons, glitter), coffee can with lid, bells, sandpaper, blocks of wood, one shoe box with lid per child, large rubber bands

Instructions:

These materials can make a variety of musical instruments. You can incorporate colors, letters, and numbers by including them in your decorations.

- **Guitar.** Decorate a shoe box, and cut a 3-to-4-inch (8-10 cm) hole in the lid. Have your child practice writing his Gs for guitar on the box top as part of the decorations. Wrap rubber bands of different widths around the box lengthwise. Be sure the rubber bands go across the hole. Strum the rubber bands to make sounds.

- **Drum.** Decorate a coffee can, and replace the lid. Use wooden spoons or small sticks to drum on the lid.

- **Bells.** Tie bells to your child's shoelaces or use yarn to attach. He can listen to the bells while he dances.
- **Paper-plate shaker.** Place two paper plates together with their top surfaces inward, and staple them almost completely shut. Add about two handfuls dried beans in the opening before stapling it shut. Decorate your shaker as you wish, and shake away. Streamers make a nice decoration for this one. It's also a good idea to have your child practice writing his *Ss* as part of the decoration.
- **Sandpaper blocks.** Cover two blocks of wood with rough sandpaper, and staple or glue down the edges. When your child rubs them together, it will make a musical sound.

Activity 4: Get Those Sounds in Order!

Skills learned: Ordering and classifying sounds by pitch or loudness
Materials: Various objects that make sounds when you drop them (e.g., spoon, cotton, plastic, wooden block, or rocks of different sizes), cookie sheet
Instructions:
Have your child drop the objects you've provided onto a cookie sheet. Help him identify the loudness of the sound each object makes—from a loud sound to no sound at all. Help him order the objects from loud to soft, and discuss why they are louder or softer (usually due to weight or material).

Activity 5: Sound Match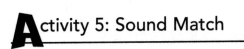

Skills learned: Discrimination of sounds
Materials: Plastic eggs or other matching containers that aren't see-through, rice, large dried beans, salt, small dried peas

Instructions:

1. Fill two containers with the same type and amount of a material (e.g., 1 tablespoon rice). Repeat with all materials and egg pairs. Divide the containers into two sets so that each set is identical.

2. Give your child a container from one set, and ask him to shake it. Tell him he needs to find the matching sounds in the other set of containers. Continue with all sounders.

Activity 6: Sound Bingo

Skills learned: Sound identification, listening, following directions, fine motor

Materials: Construction or printer paper, crayons, buttons or beans

Instructions:

1. Create several bingo cards by designing on the computer or drawing a 3-by-3-inch to 4-by-4-inch grid. (You'll have 9 or 12 squares.) On the bingo cards, draw things that make noise (e.g., bear, airplane, telephone, cat, dog) or attach clip art. On slips of paper, write the name of each item you drew, and place the labels in a bag.

2. Explain to your child that you are playing Sound Bingo. Give him a pile of buttons or beans as markers, and tell him that if he hears an object that is on his bingo card, he should cover it with a marker.

3. Draw a label out of the bag, and make the sound of the object. If your child's card has a picture of that object, then he should cover it with a marker. Be sure you play, too. The first to fill a line with markers wins!

Activity 7: Back-to-Back Directions

Skills learned: Listening, following directions, large and fine motor, cooperation

Materials: Blocks

Instructions:

1. Sit back-to-back with your child, or have two children sit back-to-back.

2. Give each an identical pile of blocks. Have them take turns being the director.

3. The director starts to build something with his blocks and tells his partner each step. Without looking, the partner must do as he's told.

4. When the structures are built, have them check each other's to see if they look alike.

Activity 8: *B* Is for *Bell*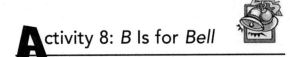

Skills learned: Writing, letter recognition and phonics (*B*), fine motor

Materials: 1 sheet of construction paper, crayon, children's safety scissors

Instructions:

1. Draw a large bell on the construction paper. Draw a handwriting practice line across the middle of the bell, and write a *B* at the beginning of the line.

2. Give your child the bell page, and have him practice writing his *B*s. Discuss the sound *B* makes and that *bell* begins with *B*.

3. Have your child cut out the bell.

Activity 9: Rhyme Hop

Skills learned: Rhyming, listening, large motor, following directions

Materials: Construction paper, crayons

Instructions:

1. Draw large pictures of objects whose names rhyme (e.g., dog, hog, log, frog, jog) and some that don't (e.g, box, man), each on its own piece of construction paper. Lay the pictures that rhyme in a path around the room, but add a few offshoots with the pictures that don't rhyme.

2. Tell your child that this is a rhyme competition. Show him the starting picture and name it. Tell him that he must hop to the picture that rhymes with the first picture (e.g., from the frog to the log). Have him continue down the path.

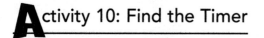ctivity 10: Find the Timer

Skills learned: Listening, following directions, large motor
Materials: Portable, ticking kitchen timer
Instructions:

1. Have your child leave the room, then wind up the kitchen timer. Hide it somewhere in the room you are in.

2. Have your child come back in and try to find the timer by listening for it.

ctivity 11: What Is That Sound?

Skills learned: Listening, identifying by sound, memory
Materials: Various common objects that make a noise (e.g., pot and lid, familiar toys that make noise, whistle), a box
Instructions:

1. Place the objects in a box. Don't let your child see them.

2. Have your child close his eyes.

3. Pull out one object at a time and make a noise with it. Ask your child what the object is. If he guesses right, he gets to keep it. See how many objects he can identify.

Review Time

- Why is it important for people to hear?
- What does a low noise sound like?
- Can you find the letter *B* in our activities?
- What sound does *B* as in *bell* make?
- What was your favorite activity in the lesson? Mine was . . .

Lesson 16

A B C D E F G H I J K L M N O P Q R S T U V W X Y Z

Sight, Taste, Smell

Featured Letters: N, S, and T

Introductory Activity: Book About the Five Senses

Skills learned: Prereading, knowledge of the five senses, reading comprehension, listening

Instructions:

1. Read aloud a book about the five senses. Ask your child some comprehension questions.

2. Take this time to discuss the five senses. Tell her that this lesson focuses on sight, taste, and smell. Ask her to tell you the different things she can see, taste, and smell.

Activity 2: Discussion About the Sense of Smell

Skills learned: Knowledge of the sense of smell

Instructions:

Sit down with your child, and ask her some questions about the sense of smell.

- What do we use to smell?
- How do we smell? Can you show me?
- What happens if you try and smell with your mouth?
- Can you name some things that smell good?
- Can you name some things that don't smell very good?

Activity 3: Match the Smells

Skills learned: Sense of smell, memory, matching

Materials: Several small bowls, cotton balls, aluminum foil, strong-smelling food items (for example, peanut butter, coffee, onion, peppermint)

Instructions:

1. Take two samples of each strong-smelling food, and put each sample in a separate bowl. Cover all the bowls with aluminum foil, and poke holes in the foil. Mix up the bowls, and put them on the table.

2. Invite your child to smell each bowl. Have her tell you what she smells and then try to find its match.

Activity 4: Nose Sequence

Skills learned: Sequencing, matching, letter recognition and phonics (N), writing, counting

Materials: Construction paper (various colors), scissors, glue (optional), crayons

Instructions:

1. Cut several noses out of construction paper of different colors. Make sure you cut several of each color.

2. Arrange the noses in a sequence—for example, two red noses, a blue nose, a green nose, and three yellow noses.

3. Give the remaining noses to your child, and have her copy the sequence that you have arranged.

4. Rearrange the sequence, and let your child do it again.

5. Let your child arrange a sequence for you to copy.

6. Let your child glue the matching sequences on a piece of construction paper or store the noses in a bag to do the activity again at a later time.

7. Draw a handwriting practice line at the bottom of the construction paper and a sample letter *N*.

8. Make sure your child understands that *N* stands for *nose*, and have her sound out the letter *N*.

9. Let your child practice writing her letter *N*s on the handwriting practice line.

Activity 5: Show Me Your Taste Buds!

Skills learned: Knowledge of sense of taste, understanding of taste buds

Materials: 1 mirror

Instructions:

1. Explain to your child about taste buds. The reason people can really enjoy their favorite foods is because of the thousands of taste buds located on the tongue.

2. Show your child the bumps on your tongue, and explain that taste buds are located in those bumps.

3. Invite your child to stand in front of a mirror and explore the taste buds in her mouth.

Note: Make sure to wash your hands before and after this activity!

Activity 6: The Nose Knows What Tastes Good

Skills learned: Understanding of the nose's role in eating
Materials: Some of your child's favorite foods
Instructions:
1. Explain to your child that her nose plays a big part in her ability to taste foods. Taste buds alone do not allow her to enjoy a salty pretzel or a sweet bowl of ice cream. Her taste buds recognize if food is bitter, sweet, sour, or salty, but her nose really enhances the actual taste. Remind her that food doesn't always taste very good when she has a cold. Her stuffy nose prevents her from tasting the food the way she normally does.
2. Have your child close her eyes, hold her nose, and take a small bite of a favorite food. See if she can tell what the food is while holding her nose. Then let her have another bite while breathing normally through her nose. Encourage her to discuss the difference in the tastes.

Activity 7: Taste Test

Skills learned: Familiarity with bitter, sweet, sour, and salty tastes
Materials: Samples of foods that are bitter, sweet, sour, and salty (see suggestions listed in instructions)

Instructions:

1. Explain that the basic tastes people recognize are bitter, sweet, sour, and salty.

2. Ask your child to list some of her favorite foods, and have her tell you what they taste like.

3. Serve up small portions of the foods you've picked. Ask your child to taste each item and tell you if it is bitter, sweet, sour, or salty.

- **Bitter.** Unsweetened chocolate or powdered cocoa
- **Sweet.** Sugar, brown sugar, cotton candy, chocolate chips
- **Sour.** Lemon
- **Salty.** Chips, pretzels

Activity 8: Guess the Taste

Skills learned: Familiarity with bitter, sweet, sour, and salty tastes
Materials: Toothpicks, 4 cups with water, lemon juice, cocoa, salt, sugar
Instructions:

1. Add the lemon juice to one cup of water, cocoa to another, salt to another, and sugar to the last.

2. Now that your child has a better understanding of the four different types of tastes, have her dip her toothpick into each cup, take a taste of the flavored water, and tell you what each one tastes like.

Activity 9: T Is for *Taste*

Skills learned: Letter recognition and phonics (*T*), fine motor
Materials: Construction paper, glue, children's safety scissors, food magazine

Instructions:

1. Draw a large block-letter *T* on the construction paper, and have your child cut it out. If she's not quite ready for scissors, cut it out for her.

2. Explain that *T* stands for *taste*. Have her make the "t" sound with you.

3. Let her flip through a food magazine and pick out different foods. Encourage her to talk about what she thinks the food would taste like (e.g., bitter, sweet, salty, sour, spicy).

4. Help her cut out the food items (or cut them out yourself).

5. Have your child glue the food items on the *T*.

Activity 10: Eyes Are Important

Skills learned: Understanding of why eyes are important; heightened sense of touch, smell, and hearing

Materials: 1 bag of microwave popcorn, portable radio or a toy that makes noise, scarf or paper grocery bag

Instructions:

1. Encourage your child to discuss several things she can see with her eyes. Have her close her eyes and picture in her mind what those things look like. Explain that some people cannot see and don't know what these things look like. People who are blind have to use their other senses to understand what an object is. Ask her questions: What would it be like if you couldn't see? How would you know where you were walking? If you couldn't see what I am making in the kitchen, how would you know what kind of food it is? Could you hear the food? Could you smell the food? How could you tell if a car was coming in the street? Could you smell the car coming? Would you hear the car coming?

2. Have your child hide in her room (or another place) while you set up a portable radio or toy to make noise somewhere else in the house.

3. Blindfold your child with the scarf. (Sometimes being blindfolded can be scary. If that's the case, let her cover her head with a paper bag or just close her eyes.)

4. Instruct your child to find the source of the noise by listening to it and feeling her way through the house. Make sure the floor is clear of obstacles and that you are always by her side to avoid any collisions or dangerous steps.

5. After she has found the object, have her hide in her room while you make the popcorn.

6. Blindfold her, have her come out of her hiding place, and ask her to tell you what is cooking in the kitchen by using her sense of smell. Let her take a small taste if she needs help.

Activity 11: Color Coordination

Skills learned: Color recognition, sorting, ordering
Materials: Bowl, paint swatches (various colors)
Instructions:

1. Pick up several paper paint swatches from a home decorating, paint, or hardware store. (The stores usually have a wall dedicated to paint swatches where you can find various colors. Each strip has about five shades of each color.) Separate the swatches on each strip by cutting them and placing them in a bowl.

2. Have your child separate all the shades by their color (e.g., all the shades of yellow go into one pile, all the shades of green into another).

3. Once the shades have been sorted according to general color, have your child sort each color from the lightest shade to the darkest. For example, put all the shades of green in front of your child and have her sort them from lightest to darkest.

Activity 12: Eyelash Match

Skills learned: Counting, number recognition, fine motor, letter recognition and phonics (*S*)

Materials: Construction paper, black pipe cleaners, glue, black marker

Instructions:

1. Draw several eye shapes on the construction paper. Draw a circle for each pupil, and write a different number in each eye. Choose numbers that you are currently working on with your child.

2. Cut the pipe cleaners. They will be eyelashes for the eyes, so make the lashes proportional to the eye.

3. Have your child identify the number in each eye and then glue the same number of eyelashes around the eye. For example, if an eye has the number 8, then your child will count out eight pieces of pipe cleaner and glue them around the eye.

4. Draw a handwriting practice line on the construction paper, and write a sample *S*. Explain that *S* stands for *see*. Have her make the "s" sound with you.

5. Have your child practice writing her *S*s on the handwriting line.

Activity 13: Peanut Butter and Jelly by Touch

Skills learned: Fine motor, understanding why eyes are important, heightened sense of touch

Materials: Peanut butter, jelly, bread, paper plate, spreading knife (or any knife that is not serrated), blindfold

Instructions:

1. Place all the materials for making peanut butter and jelly sandwiches on a table, and have your child sit at the table.

2. Blindfold your child and have her make a peanut butter and jelly sandwich by touch only. Help her feel around for things safely. This activity is best performed sitting down. Don't use stools at a counter, as she could lose her balance and fall.

3. When she is finished with the task, ask her what it was like. Encourage her to discuss if it was easy or hard and what senses she had to rely on to make the sandwich.

Variation:

For a less messy alternative, or for children with an allergy to peanuts, have your child try and get dressed in the dark.

Review Time

- What senses would you use if you couldn't see?
- What senses would you use if you couldn't hear?
- What things taste good to you?
- Can you find the letters *N*, *S*, and *T* in our activities?
- What sounds do *N* as in *nose* and *T* as in *taste* make?
- What was your favorite part of the lesson? Mine was . . .

Lesson 17

Touch

Featured Letters: H and Your Child's Name

Introductory Activity: Book About Hands and Touch

Skills learned: Prereading, listening, reading comprehension, knowledge of sense of touch

Instructions:

1. Read aloud a book about hands and the sense of touch to your child. Ask your child questions about the story you read to check for comprehension.

2. Be sure to discuss the different things people's hands can do (e.g., squeeze, test for temperature, feel textures, hold, balance objects, manipulate).

3. Part of our hands are our fingers. Sing:

Where Is Pointer? (traditional song sung to the tune of "Frére Jacques")
Where is thumbkin? (Hold fists closed.)
Where is thumbkin?
Here I am. (Hold up and wiggle right thumb.)

Here I am. (Hold up and wiggle left thumb.)
How are you today, sir? (Wiggle right thumb.)
Very well, I thank you. (Wiggle left thumb.)
Run away. (Hide right thumb.)
Run away. (Hide left thumb.)
(Repeat with ring man, tall man, pointer, and pinky.)

Activity 2: What Are Hands For?

Skills learned: Sense of touch, fine motor, rhyming, rhythm
Materials: Water, fabric of choice, 2 potatoes, glue, play dough, clothespins, calculator
Instructions:
1. Dampen one end of the fabric, and warm up a potato in the microwave.
2. Discuss with your child that you have five senses, what they are (touch, sight, hearing, taste, and smell), and that today's lesson is about the sense of touch.
3. Give your child the play dough to explore and squeeze, some clothespins to pinch, and calculator buttons to press. Let him feel a warm and cold potato. Have him close his eyes and decide what part of the fabric is wet or dry.
4. We can do all these things and more with our hands. Ask your child, "What are other things you do with your hands?"

Activity 3: If We Didn't Have Hands

Skills learned: Fine motor, large motor, problem solving
Materials: Small rocks or marbles, bucket or bowl, thumbtack with a tall head, masking tape

Instructions:

1. Display the bucket and several marbles on the floor next to it. Ask, "What if we didn't have hands, and I asked you to move these marbles into the bucket? How could you do it?" Let your child brainstorm and try different methods such as moving the marbles with his toes or squeezing his elbows together. Do not let him use his mouth. Be sure to put the marbles out of your child's reach once the activity is over.

2. Tape your child's thumb to his pointer finger. Show him a thumbtack stuck into the wall or bulletin board. Ask him to remove the tack with his hand but without his thumb. Why is this hard? Conclude that our entire hand is very useful.

Activity 4: Opposites

Skills learned: Matching opposites, sense of touch
Materials: Various materials with opposite textures
Instructions:

1. Gather together various materials with opposite textures (e.g., rough and smooth, bumpy and silky, dry and wet).

2. Display the different materials in front of your child. Let him touch the materials and describe how they feel. Discuss what *opposite* means (e.g., rough and smooth).

3. Give him one of the materials, and ask him to describe it.

4. Ask him to find a material with the opposite texture.

5. Continue with all of the matches.

Activity 5: Which Is Different?

Skills learned: Sense of touch, knowledge of difference

Materials: Various materials with different textures (e.g., silk, burlap, double-sided tape, foil), construction paper, glue, blindfold (optional)

Instructions:

1. Pick one textured material, and cut out three 2-inch (5 cm) samples. Choose a different textured material, and cut one sample of it. Glue these four samples in a row on a sheet of construction paper. Be sure the samples are in random order (e.g, rough, rough, smooth, rough).

2. Repeat the preceding process with at least three more rows.

3. Have your child close his eyes, or blindfold him.

4. Ask him to feel a row of textured material and tell you which one is different, based on how they feel. Repeat with the other rows of material.

Activity 6: Hand Bake

Skills learned: Knowledge of growth, large motor, writing, letter and number recognition, name recognition

Materials: Baker's clay (available at craft stores), oven, rolling pin, cookie sheet, skewer or screwdriver, paint (optional), wax paper

Instructions:

1. Discuss with your child that he is growing and so are his hands. (If you have a print of his hand when he was born, show it to him.) Today you are going to make a print of his hand so that both of you will always remember what it looked like.

2. Provide your child with a hunk of baker's clay, and help him press it into a large circle on some wax paper. He may need a rolling pin to smooth it out. A smooth cup turned on its side works, too.

3. Press his hand into the circle to make a print, and help him carve his name and the date into the circle with the skewer. Be sure to use safety precautions when handling the skewer or any pointy tool.

4. Move the clay to a cookie sheet and bake as directed. Paint if desired.

Activity 7: Shape and Name Rubbings

Skills learned: Prewriting, sense of touch, fine motor, shapes, name and letter recognition, rhythm

Materials: Paper doilies, sandpaper, a dark crayon with the paper removed, masking tape, sheet of plain paper, scissors

Instructions:

1. Cut the doilies into various shapes and the sandpaper into the letters of your child's name.

2. Tape the paper doily pieces and sandpaper letters on a table.

3. Have your child place his sheet of plain paper over the pieces and then use the side of his crayon to rub the paper. The shapes from underneath should appear on the paper.

4. Discuss why the shapes and letters show up as they do (texture) and what the shapes and letters are. Sing "The Name Song" from "Lesson 1: All About Me."

Activity 8: Paper Bag Puppets

Skills learned: Creativity, dramatic play, fine motor, shapes, colors

Materials: Small paper lunch sack, construction paper, glue, scissors, black marker, google eyes (optional), pipe cleaners (optional)

Instructions:

1. Cut multiple shapes from the construction paper. Keep in mind that these shapes will be puppet features and should be sized accordingly.

2. Show your child how sliding his hand into the open end of a paper lunch bag and wrapping his fingers around the fold at the bottom can make the bag into a talking puppet.

3. Give your child the pile of shapes and decorations, Let him create a puppet. It can be an animal, monster, or whatever he chooses.

4. Make one for yourself. Then put on a puppet show.

Activity 9: Paper Plate Numbers

Skills learned: Fine motor, recognition of numbers
Materials: Paper plates, black marker, clothespins
Instructions:

1. Write a number in the middle of each paper plate. You may use as many paper plates as you choose. Give your child a pile of clothespins, and have him pinch the pins open and place the appropriate number of pins around the paper plate. This exercise will help your child strengthen his fine motor muscles, so it is important that he does the pinching.

2. If your child is just learning to count, you may draw the appropriate number of dots around each plate for your child to clip onto and count.

Activity 10: Magic Hands

Skills learned: Fine motor, letter recognition and phonics (*H*), writing
Materials: White construction paper, washable watercolor paints, paintbrush, water in a glass for rinsing paintbrush, white crayon

Instructions:

1. Have your child lay his hand on the white construction paper. Help him trace around his hand with the white crayon.

2. Help him write *H*s on the top of the paper with the white crayon.

3. Have him paint the entire paper with the watercolors. His hand and *H*s should magically appear.

Activity 11: Sponge Relay

Skills learned: Fine motor, following directions, large motor, knowledge of absorption

Materials: Large sponges, water, several buckets or bowls

Instructions:

1. This activity should be done outdoors. Fill a bucket or bowl with water for each child. Place a smaller bowl or bucket 3 to 10 feet (1–3 m) away, depending on how hard you want to make the activity.

2. Give your child a sponge, and explain that he has to use the sponge to soak up water in the large bucket and then transfer it to the small bucket. You can make it a race where the first one to fill up his small bucket wins. Demonstrate first.

Review Time

- What are some important things we do with our hands?
- Can you find the letter *H* in our activities?
- Show him the project in Activity 5 and ask him to identify some different textures.
- What sound does *H* as in *hand* make?
- What was your favorite part of the lesson? Mine was . . .

Lesson 18

A B C D E F G H I J K L M N O P Q R S T U V W X Y Z

Friends

Featured Letters: F and Q

Introductory Activity: Book About Friends

Skills learned: Prereading, knowledge of having friends, reading comprehension, listening

Instructions:

1. Read aloud a book about friends, and ask some comprehension questions.

2. Ask your child the different things she can do to be a good friend.

3. Ask her if her friends always like doing the same things she does. What are some things she likes to do, and what are some things her friends like to do? Are they the same or different?

4. Have her list all of her friends (including family, neighbors, and classmates).

5. Invite a friend. This is a great lesson for two or more kids to do together.

Activity 2: Friendship Quilt

Skills learned: Letter recognition and phonics (*F* and *Q*), counting, creativity, fine motor

Materials: 4 pieces of construction paper (various colors), glitter glue or sequins, yarn, hole punch, craft accessories (e.g., stickers, stamps, sponge paint)

Instructions:

1. Line up two pieces of construction paper. Then line up the other two pieces directly underneath the first two, forming a two-by-two rectangle. Punch holes on the inside edges of each piece of construction paper. Your child will use the yarn to string the paper together, making a quilt.

2. On one of the pieces of construction paper, write your child's name, on another piece write "Friendship Quilt," and on the third piece write a number that you and your child are currently working on.

3. Have your child pick the name of a friend she likes playing with and write that friend's name on the fourth piece of paper.

4. Have your child string the quilt together with yarn. (Tape the quilt pieces together so it will be easier to string, and remove the tape after she's finished.)

5. Let her decorate her name and her friend's name with the craft accessories.

6. On the numbered quilt piece, have your child put the corresponding number of glitter-glue dots around the written number you are working on currently. For example, if you write the number 14, she'll make fourteen dots.

7. Draw two handwriting practice lines on the quilt piece that has the words "Friendship Quilt." Write a sample *F* on one and a sample *Q* on the other.

8. Have your child sound out the letters *F* and *Q* with you. If she's ready to start writing, let her practice making the letters *F* and *Q* with a pencil. If she's not quite ready to write, have her think of other words that start with the letters *F* and *Q*, which you can write down for her.

Activity 3: Name Card Decorations

Skills learned: Patterns, fine motor, concept of giving
Materials: Stickers, black marker, construction paper, craft accessories (e.g., crayons, stamps, glitter glue)
Instructions:
1. Have your child think of a friend for whom she would like to decorate a name card. Write that child's name on the construction paper.
2. Using the stickers, have your child make a patterned border. For example, if the stickers are different-colored flowers, have her do two blue flowers and then an orange flower. This pattern should go all the way around the edge of the construction paper.
3. Let your child decorate the name card with the craft accessories.
4. Have your child present the name card to her friend.

Activity 4: Interview a Friend

Skills learned: Learning that other people like different things, life skills
Materials: Pencil, writing paper
Instructions:
1. On the piece of paper, write or type the list of questions that follows these instructions.
2. Have your child interview the friend she invited to this lesson.

3. Whisper the questions in your child's ear so she can ask her friend. Record the responses.

4. Let the other child interview your child, too.

5. Take this time to discuss that everyone likes different things. Compare their answers, and watch them giggle!

- What is your favorite color?
- What is your favorite shape?
- What is your favorite toy?
- What is your favorite food?
- What is your favorite animal?
- How many pets does your family have?
- In what month is your birthday?
- How old are you?
- Do you like warm weather or cold weather?
- What is your favorite thing to do during the day?
- What is your favorite dessert?

Activity 5: Side by Side

Skills learned: Sharing, listening, fine motor, creativity, colors

Materials: 2 large pieces of construction paper, masking tape, various craft accessories (e.g., stickers, stamps, shape cutouts), glue

Instructions:

1. This is also an excellent craft for your child to do with a friend.

2. Place the two pieces of construction paper side by side, and tape them together along the seam. Masking tape works best because it doesn't tear when you pull it off the paper.

3. At the top of the paper write, "To my friend, (insert friend's name)" and at the bottom write, "Love, (insert your child's name)." Do the same on the other piece of paper and write, "To: (your child)" and "From: (her friend)."

4. Put the paper on the floor with all of the craft accessories.

5. Instruct the children to decorate the paper for each other. Before you start, let them discuss the crafts and colors that each likes best.

6. Tell them they have to share the crafts and work nicely in this small space. You are not allowed to help (unless they need it). Just leave the creativity up to the kids. Remind them that they should decorate the paper according to what their friend would like, not necessarily what they themselves would like.

Activity 6: Friendship Wreath

Skills learned: Letter recognition and phonics (*F*), writing, fine motor, colors, shapes

Materials: Tempera paint, construction paper, children's safety scissors, yarn, hole punch, crayon

Instructions:

1. Cut a large circle out of the construction paper, or supervise while your child cuts.

2. Cut another circle out of the center to make a wreath.

3. Let your child put the palm of her hand in the paint and stamp her hand onto the wreath until the wreath is completely covered with her handprints.

4. Punch a hole in the wreath, and let her string the yarn through so the wreath can be hung.

5. Sound out the letter *F* with her, and help her write a large *F* at the top.

6. Have her present it to a friend as a gift of friendship.

Variation:

1. For a different way to do the activity, invite some of her friends over and give each child a blank wreath.

2. Let them put their handprints on each wreath. Then when the craft is finished, each child has a wreath with everyone's handprints.

3. After the wreaths dry, print each child's name on one of their handprints.

Activity 7: Friendship Letter

Skills learned: Memory, writing, fine motor, sharing, knowledge of mail

Materials: Stationery, stamped envelope, decorative stickers, pen

Instructions:

1. Have your child choose a friend to send a letter to.

2. Let your child dictate to you a letter to her special friend.

3. If she needs help, encourage her to talk about the things she likes best about her friend, what makes that friend special, and what they like to do together.

4. Let your child sign her name and decorate the stationery and envelope with stickers. Address the envelope, and let your child help you mail it.

Activity 8: Friendship Maze

Skills learned: Prewriting, fine motor, logic

Materials: Paper, pencil, picture of your child, picture of your child's friend

Instructions:

1. Make a simple maze with a start, a finish, and some dead ends. (Maze templates can be found on the Internet if you prefer not to draw one.)

2. Put a picture of your child at the start and a picture of your child's friend at the finish. Give the pencil to your child, and let her navigate her way through the maze to find her friend.

Activity 9: Friendship Song

Skills learned: Rhythm, rhyming, memory, large motor

Instructions:

1. While clapping in time, sing with your child the song that follows these instructions.

2. Have your child clap, too.

3. Sing the song again, and let your child choose something to do instead of clapping.

4. Take turns coming up with different things to do while singing the song (e.g., jumping, stomping, hopping on one foot, patting your nose).

> *Friends Song (to the tune of "Row, Row, Row Your Boat")*
> Friends, friends, friends are great.
> They're warm just like the sun.
> We sing and play and dance all day.
> Can't wait to have more fun.

Review Time

- Can you name some of your friends?
- What makes your friends special?
- Can you find the letters *F* and *Q* in our activities?
- What sounds do *F* as in *friendship* and *Q* as in *quilt* make?
- What crafts will you be giving to a friend?
- What was your favorite part of the lesson? Mine was . . .

Lesson 19

ABCDEFGHIJKLMNOPQRSTUVWXYZ

Fire and Stranger Safety

Featured Letters: D, R, and S

Introductory Activity: Book About Fires and Firemen

Skills learned: Prereading, listening, knowledge of firemen, reading comprehension

Instructions:

1. Read the book aloud to your child, and ask comprehension questions about the particular story you read.

2. Discuss what firemen do, how fires can be avoided, and other related questions.

Activity 2: Dalmatian Math

Skills learned: Number recognition, counting

Materials: White paper, construction-paper squares, black marker, masking tape

Instructions:

1. Draw plain white dalmatians on the paper, or get them from clip art or online coloring pages. Fill in the dogs' spots according to the numbers you are working on. For example, if you are working on the number six, put six spots on a dog.

2. On the construction-paper squares, put numerals that correspond to the number of dots on the dogs.

3. Place masking tape on the reverse side of each dog and number square.

4. Display the numbers on a felt board and have your child match the dogs to the numbers based on the number of spots.

Activity 3: Fireman's Hose Ordering

Skills learned: Ordering by size and number, knowledge of firemen

Materials: Cream or gray construction paper, scissors, black marker

Instructions:

1. Cut five fire hoses (long and snaky shapes) out of the construction paper. Each hose should be a different length. Choose five consecutive numbers and write each number on a hose (for example, 1, 2, 3, 4, 5). Be sure the consecutive numbers are not in the same order as the sizes.

2. Discuss with your child that firemen use fire hoses to get water to the fire they are trying to put out.

3. Give your child the hoses, and have him order them by size. Then have him order the hoses by increasing and decreasing numbers.

Activity 4: Safety Item Memory

Skills learned: Knowledge of firemen and safety items, memory

Materials: Construction paper; computer clip art, online coloring pages, or magazine clippings; scissors; dish towel

Instructions:

1. Cut five to ten squares of construction paper.

2. Draw pictures of safety items such as a fire hose, fireman's helmet, smoke alarm, fire extinguisher, fire truck, ambulance, or policeman on the squares. If you don't want to draw the safety items, find clip art or online coloring pages to glue on the squares.

3. Display all the pictures of the safety items in front of your child, and explain to him what each item is and what it's used for. Collect the pictures into a pile.

4. Lay four pictures in front of your child for about twenty seconds. Have him look closely at the pictures and try to remember the safety items he is seeing.

5. Cover the pictures up with the dish towel, and ask your child to tell you all the safety items he remembers.

6. Do this again with another set of pictures. Display more pictures for added difficulty.

Activity 5: Fire Art

Skills learned: Fine motor, colors and color mixing, shapes, social skills

Materials: Tempera paint (black, orange, red, and yellow), 2 pieces of black construction paper, glue, children's safety scissors, wax paper, white chalk, black marker

Instructions:

1. Have your child squeeze out large dollops of orange, red, and yellow paint onto the construction paper. Add about 5 drops of black paint. You want enough paint to mix together and cover the paper.

2. Place a large piece of wax paper over the paint on the paper, and have your child press the paper down and wiggle it. The paint will blend together.

3. Pull up the wax paper with a strong upward motion. This will cause the paint to form peaks and look more like fire.

4. Draw a tree and house on the black paper with the white chalk. When the paint dries, have your child cut out the house and trees from the construction paper and glue them over the paint. You could also make a black cutout of a fire truck. (Outlines are available if you look up coloring pages of fire trucks online.)

5. Write "FIRE" on the paper with a black marker.

Variation:

1. For a lesson in giving, have your child repeat the craft and turn it into a thank-you note for the firefighters at your local station. Thank them for all the hard work they do. Make sure your child signs his name.

2. When you go on a field trip to the fire station, present the note to the firefighters.

Activity 6: Escape from the Smoke

Skills learned: Large motor, rhythm, knowledge of escaping a fire and smoke, color and letter recognition (optional)

Materials: Several bedsheets, clothespins or yarn, chairs, construction paper (optional), red marker (optional), see-through scarf or other see-through material for covering your child's eyes

Instructions:

1. Make a very low canopy with the sheets. Attach the sheets to chairs or other pieces of furniture.

2. Explain to your child that smoke from a fire can prevent him from breathing because it is so thick. Smoke also makes it hard to see in a fire. There is less smoke down on the ground when there is a fire, because smoke rises. So it is best to crawl on the floor to get out of a smoky room.

3. Cover your child's eyes with the see-through scarf. This will help diminish his eyesight. If this is too scary, omit this step.

4. The sheets are pretend smoke. Have him crawl from one side of the darkened room to the other by going under the sheets.

Variation:

1. For a greater challenge, write "HOT" in large, red letters on a piece of construction paper.

2. Discuss with your child that in a fire certain areas of the house will be too hot for him to go through. He should always feel a door for heat before opening it. If one way out is blocked by heat, he should find another way out.

3. As your child crawls out of the "smoke" sheets, flash him the construction paper that says "HOT." Tell your child, "Too hot!" Your child must find another way out.

Activity 7: Escape

Skills learned: Large motor, safety, rhyming, rhythm

Instructions:

1. Discuss at length fire safety and getting out of the house. Make a fire escape plan, and designate a meeting place. Let your child listen to the smoke alarm so that he won't be frightened if he hears it.

2. Practice! Have your child lie in bed like he is sleeping, and tell him you are going to set the fire alarm off. Tell him that this is only a drill and that in a drill there is no real fire. You want him to pretend there is a fire and follow your fire escape plan. Remind him to stay low to the ground as he gets out of the house. Staying low is how people avoid smoke. Walk him through the drill, and then have him attempt it on his own. Sing as you practice:

> *Fire Escape Song (to the tune of "The Ants Go Marching")*
> If there's a fire inside your house, get out! Get out!
> If there's a fire inside your house, get out! Get out!
> Save playtime for another day.
> Crawl down low. That is the way.
> And get out of your house *right away*!

Activity 8: Stop, Drop, and Roll

Skills learned: Large motor, knowledge of how to put out flames on one's body, rhythm, letter recognition and phonics (*D*, *S*, *R*)
Materials: Red felt, construction paper, flannel shirt, masking tape
Instructions:

1. Cut out flames from the red felt. Cut out a large *S*, *D*, and *R* from the construction paper. Tape the letters on the floor in this order: *S*, *D*, and then *R* a few feet away.

2. Tell your child that the best way to put out flames on his body is to stop, drop, and roll. *S* stands for *stop*, *D* stands for *drop*, and *R* stands for *roll*. Emphasize the letter sounds as you work. Demonstrate stopping on the *S*, dropping on the *D*, and rolling on the *R* for your child. Explain to him that rolling on the ground smothers the fire.

3. Place the shirt on your child and then stick the felt flames onto it. Tell your child, "Oh, no! You're on fire! What should you do?"

4. Have your child stop, drop, and roll on the *S*, *D*, and *R*. The flames should come off while he is rolling around. "Whew! You did it!"

5. Sing the following song while you practice:

Stop, Drop, and Roll (to the tune of "Bingo")

If you find your clothes on fire, what should you do-oh?

Stop! *Stop!* Drop and roll.

Stop! *Stop!* Drop and roll.

Stop! *Stop!* Drop and roll.

That is what you should do-oh.

Activity 9: What Is a Stranger?

Skills learned: Fine motor, knowledge of who is and who is not a stranger, prereading, listening, letter recognition and phonics (*D*), writing

Materials: Pictures of people your child knows and is safe with, pictures cut from magazines of people your child doesn't know (sinister looking and not), pictures of firemen and policemen, large poster board, black marker, glue, the book *Little Red Riding Hood*

Instructions:

1. Title your poster board, "What Is a Stranger?" Divide the poster board in half with a line, and label one side "Safe" and the other side "Danger." Draw a handwriting practice line at the bottom of the paper, and write a sample *D* at the beginning of it.

2. Read aloud *Little Red Riding Hood*. Be sure to discuss that Little Red Riding Hood got into trouble because she spoke with someone she didn't know while her parents weren't around. Talk about strangers and why it's important not to speak with them.

3. Help your child decide what pictures show a stranger and what pictures show someone safe. How far you take this discussion depends on the maturity of your child. Remind your child that not every stranger looks scary. Some people may look like a mommy or a daddy, but your child still should not ever go with someone he doesn't know. Be sure to explain, too, that policemen and firemen aren't strangers, but are there to help us.

4. Have your child glue the pictures of strangers under the word *danger* and the people whom he can trust under the word *safe*.

5. Have your child practice writing his *D*s for *danger* on the handwriting line.

Activity 10: Stranger Danger Practice

Skills learned: Large motor, knowledge of how to deal with strangers, social skills

Instructions:

1. Practice scenarios with your child where you pretend to be a stranger. Demonstrate for your child what he should say and do if a stranger tries to get him to go anywhere. Give your child permission to scream and call for help. It is very important that your child knows he can be rude. Have him practice hollering, "No!" Tell him that if someone is trying to forcefully take him, he should scream, hit, or kick—whatever it takes to get away. Children are told so often not to be rude and not to hit that they need to hear you say it is okay to shed the manners if they feel they are in danger.

2. This activity may be a little scary for your child, but it is very important. When I (Tara) first pretended to be a stranger for my child and asked him to come with me to get some candy, he said, "Okay." I was shocked because we had just discussed never leaving with a stranger. We had to really talk about the fact that there are bad people and that he must *never* go away with someone he doesn't know—even if they seem nice.

3. Practice scenarios such as, "Go with me and I'll give you candy," "Come over and see my puppy," "Your mom is sick and wants me to take you to her," or "Could you give me directions?" This, of course, depends on the maturity of your child, but you can't ignore this issue. Bad people are out there!

Activity 11: Ladder Exercises

Skills learned: Large motor, number recognition, addition, subtraction

Materials: Masking tape or a simple wooden ladder, construction paper, black marker

Instructions:

1. Create a ladder on your floor using masking tape. You can also use a real ladder as long as the rungs are easy to walk between. Simply lay the ladder down on the floor. Cut out construction-paper squares, and tape them onto the rungs of the ladder. On each square, write a number from a consecutive series (e.g., 4, 5, 6, 7, 8).

2. Have your child hop or step between the rungs of the ladder. If you are using an actual ladder, your child can step between the rungs or crawl on his feet and hands like a bear across the rungs to simulate climbing the ladder.

3. As your child crawls, hops, or steps, have him name the numbers he is stepping over. Then ask him to reverse his direction so that he has counted both up and down.

4. For addition and subtraction practice, have your child step two rungs up the ladder. Then ask him to step up two more. How many rungs has he climbed in all? Continue with similar exercises.

Activity 12: Fire Station Visit

Skills learned: Large motor, knowledge of firemen and their job, social skills, knowledge of community

Instructions:

1. Call your local fire department, and set up a time for you and your child to visit. Most fire stations give free tours to kids and show them the equipment.

2. Make sure to ask the firemen to model the fire suit for your child. Firemen look pretty scary in the suits, and you don't want your child to hide from a fireman if your child ever needs one. Visiting a fire department is a great thing to do at least once a year.

Review Time

- Fire safety and stranger safety is *so* important, and it is never too early to start talking about these things with your kids.

- Frequently ask your child, "What is your full name? What are your parent's names?"

- Remember to make up songs about your child's address and phone number. You may make it a habit to sing your family's address song every time you come home together.

- What do you do if someone you don't know asks you to go off with him or her?

- What do you do if there is a fire in our house? If you hear the smoke alarm?

- Can you find the letters *D*, *S*, and *R* in our activities?

- What sound does *D* as in *danger* make?

- What was your favorite part of the this lesson? Mine was . . .

Rainbows

Featured Letters: B, G, O, P, R, V, and Y

Introductory Activity: Rainbow or Noah's Ark Book

Skills learned: Prereading, listening, reading comprehension, knowledge of rainbows

Instructions:

1. Read aloud a rainbow or Noah's ark book to your child. Be sure to ask comprehension questions about the story you chose.

2. Discuss that rainbows follow rain as a promise from God that he will never flood the earth again, or discuss rainbows from a scientific perspective.

Activity 2: Rainbow Mosaic Art and Song

Skills learned: Knowledge of rainbows, colors, fine motor, letter recognition and phonics (*R*), writing, rhyming

Materials: Construction paper (rainbow colors: white, red, orange, yellow, green, blue, purple), marker, glue, children's safety scissors, cotton balls

Instructions:

1. Draw a large rainbow on a sheet of white construction paper with seven lines, each about 1 inch apart. Cut a 1-inch (2.5 cm) strip of paper from each color of construction paper.

2. Give your child the rainbow picture and color strips. Have her cut or tear each strip into 1- to 2-inch (2.5 to 5 cm) pieces.

3. Teach this rainbow color poem to your child for learning color order:

Rainbow

Rainbow red and orange and yellow,

Rainbow green and blue, my fellow,

Purple is the very end

Of this beautiful rainbow God did send. (*Or*, Of this beautiful rainbow rain did send.)

4. Have her glue the colored pieces of paper onto the appropriate rainbow lines.

5. Give your child several cotton balls, and have her stretch them apart to look like clouds. Have her glue the "clouds" around the base of the rainbow.

6. At the bottom of the page, draw a handwriting practice line and write a sample *R* for your child. Have her practice writing her *R*s on the line. Discuss *R*s sound as in *rainbow*.

Activity 3: Patterned Necklace

Skills learned: Patterning, fine motor, colors

Materials: Uncooked penne noodles, food coloring to make rainbow colors, rubbing alcohol, paper towels, yarn

Instructions:

1. To dye the noodles the colors of the rainbow (red, orange, yellow, green, blue, and purple), put them into six separate bowls and cover them with rubbing alcohol mixed with food coloring. Soak the noodles until they are the colors you desire. Dry the noodles on paper towels for several hours.

2. Take a piece of yarn and start a colored-noodle pattern on it. Give it to your child and have her continue the pattern to create a necklace. Be sure to let her string the noodles.

Activity 4: Rainbow Puzzle

Skills learned: Colors of the rainbow, logic
Materials: White construction paper, crayons (rainbow colors), scissors
Instructions:

1. Draw a large rainbow on the white paper. The rainbow should have six wide sections. Color the sections in this order: red, orange, yellow, green, blue, and purple. Cut out the rainbow; then cut out each colored section of the rainbow.

2. Give your child the mixed-up rainbow sections, and have her piece the rainbow puzzle back together. She should be able to do this based on the size of each arc. For example, the top arc will be the largest.

Activity 5: Which Color Is Missing?

Skills learned: Visual discrimination, colors of rainbow
Materials: Felt (rainbow colors), scissors, felt board

Instructions:

1. Cut out a rectangle from each color of felt.

2. Display these on the felt board in order: red, orange, yellow, green, blue, and purple.

3. Now have your child cover her eyes and remove one rectangle. Then have her uncover her eyes and tell you which color is missing. Do this several times.

Activity 6: Dark-to-Light Color Chart

Skills learned: Colors, ordering from dark to light, sorting, letter recognition and phonics (*B, G, O, P, R, Y*)

Materials: Poster board or large construction paper, white paper rectangles colored with three shades of each rainbow color (e.g., pink, red, dark red), glue

Instructions:

1. Title your poster board "Rainbow Shades," and draw the following table:

	Red	*Orange*	*Yellow*	*Green*	*Blue*	*Purple*
Light						
Medium						
Dark						

2. Give your child the rectangles in one pile. Ask her to separate the pile into the different colors. Ask her to identify the colors.

3. Have her put the rectangle squares in order from light to dark and glue each in its correct column. She can find where to place each color by finding the correct beginning letter for each color word.

Activity 7: Milky Rainbows

Skills learned: Fine motor, colors, knowledge of density of liquids

Materials: Red, blue, and yellow food coloring; dishwashing liquid; clear pie plate; whole milk

Instructions:

1. Fill the pie plate halfway with whole milk.

2. Have your child *gently* squeeze three to five drops each of red, blue, and yellow food coloring into the milk, spreading the drops apart.

3. Observe that the colors don't spread out. This is because milk contains tiny drops of fat. Fat is very thick, so it holds the thin watery color in place.

4. Next have your child drizzle dishwashing liquid around the edge of the pie plate.

5. Observe the colors mixing, and discuss that the slippery soap breaks up the fatty milk, giving the thin colors room to move around and mix together.

6. Discuss the new colors that appear when the red, blue, and yellow mix.

Activity 8: Rainbow Mixing

Skills learned: Fine motor, color mixing

Materials: Ice-cube tray, liquid food coloring, eyedroppers, black permanent marker

Instructions:

1. Using the marker, write an *R*, *O*, *Y*, *G*, *B*, and *P* into separate sections of the ice tray.

2. Help your child fill the ice-cube tray half full of water.

3. Have her find the *R* cube for red and make it red with the coloring. Continue with yellow and blue.

4. Show her how to use the eyedroppers to transfer color from one cube to another.

5. Ask her how to make green, orange, and purple. You may help her make the *O* cube orange, the *G* cube green and the *P* cube purple. Let her play mix also.

Activity 9: Finger Paint Fun

Skills learned: Color mixing, fine and large motor, sense of touch
Materials: Red, blue, and yellow washable finger paints; finger-paint paper; smock; 3 zipper bags
Instructions:

1. Show your child the primary-color finger paints, and talk about what colors she sees. Tell her that these colors are called primary colors because no other colors can make these colors. But what will happen when these colors mix? Mixing primary colors creates secondary colors.

2. Experiment by putting a dollop of red paint into one of the sandwich bags. Ask your child what she thinks will happen when you add some yellow paint. Add yellow paint, squeeze the air out of the bag, and seal it. Have your child manipulate the bag and squish the paint around to mix it. What happens? She has made orange paint.

3. Do this with red and blue as well as blue and yellow.

4. Now let her finger paint with the primary and secondary colors that she made.

Activity 10: *V* Is for *Violet*

Skills learned: Letter recognition and phonics (*V*), writing, fine motor, colors

Materials: Purple construction paper, white chalk, children's safety scissors

Instructions:

1. Draw a large circle on the purple paper with the chalk. Draw a handwriting practice line across the circle, and write a sample *V* at the beginning of it.

2. Give your child the paper, and have her cut out the circle. Discuss with her that another name for purple is *violet*, and it starts with *V*. Practice the "v" sound.

3. Help her practice writing her *V*s on the handwriting practice line.

Review Time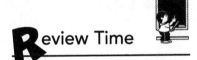

- Can you name the colors of the rainbow?
- What color do you get if you mix red and yellow?
- Can you find the letters *B*, *G*, *O*, *P*, *R*, *V*, and *Y* in our activities?
- Can you show me something light blue? Dark blue?
- What sound does *V* as in *violet* make?
- What was your favorite part of the lesson? Mine was . . .

Circus

Featured Letters: C, E, and P

Introductory Activity: Circus Book

Skills learned: Knowledge of the circus, prereading, reading comprehension, listening

Instructions:

1. Read aloud a book about the circus, and ask your child some comprehension questions.

2. Take this time to discuss the circus. Encourage your child to talk about the different animals he might see at the circus.

Activity 2: Animal Sizes

Skills learned: Ordering by size, fine motor

Materials: Pictures of circus animals (varying sizes), felt board (optional)

Instructions:

1. Place the animals on the board or in front of your child. Invite her to line up the animals from left to right according to size.

2. Have her go from smallest to largest and vice versa.

Activity 3: Elephant Balloon Paint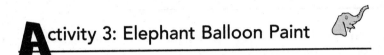

Skills learned: Fine motor skills, letter recognition and phonics (*E*), mixing colors

Materials: Coloring page of an elephant, card stock, scissors, black and white paint, paper plate, 1 balloon, glue, 1 piece of construction paper, crayon

Instructions:

1. Find a coloring page of an elephant on the Internet. It's best to print it on card stock rather than printer paper.

2. Cut out the elephant.

3. Ask your child what he thinks will happen when you mix black and white paint. Then let him help you mix a little black paint with white paint to make gray on a paper plate.

4. Blow up the balloon a little bigger than a tennis ball. Your child should be able to hold it easily and apply pressure to it without popping it.

5. Place the elephant in front of your child, and give him the paint and balloon.

6. Instruct him to dab the balloon into the paint and then dab the balloon onto the elephant. He should cover the entire elephant with paint by using this dabbing motion. After the paint dries, it should look like real elephant skin.

7. Have your child glue the elephant onto the construction paper. Write "ELEPHANT" across the top of the page. Have him sound out the letter E.

8. Give him a crayon, and help him write the letter *E*. Let him try decorating the rest of the paper with the letter *E*.

Activity 4: *P* Is for *Popcorn*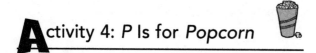

Skills learned: Letter recognition and phonics (*P*), fine motor
Materials: Card stock, black marker, popcorn kernels, glue, tweezers (optional)
Instructions:
1. Draw a large black letter *P* on card stock.
2. Make sure your child knows that *P* stands for *popcorn*. Have her sound out the letter *P*.
3. Let your child glue the popcorn kernels on the letter *P*. Either she can pinch one at a time or you can let her use the tweezers with supervision for a more challenging activity.

Activity 5: Popcorn Bags

Skills learned: Fine motor, phonics, counting
Materials: 1 paper lunch bag, red construction paper, glue, children's safety scissors
Instructions:
1. Draw 1-inch-wide strips on the red construction paper. The strips should be the same length as the bag.
2. Have your child cut the strips with the safety scissors.
3. Let your child glue the strips onto the bag about 1 inch apart.
4. Have your child count the number of strips he glued onto the bag.
5. Have your child sound out the word *popcorn* with you. Write the letters on the bag as you both sound them out.

6. After the glue dries, make a tasty bag of popcorn to share.

Variation:

1. For a greater challenge, instead of writing down the letters in Step 5, use precut construction-paper letters, which you can find at craft and scrapbook stores.

2. Sound out each letter of the word *popcorn* with your child, and have him locate the letter and glue it to the popcorn bag.

Activity 6: Popcorn Math

Skills learned: Counting, addition, number recognition, fine motor

Materials: Construction paper, glue, popcorn kernels

Instructions:

1. Write some very simple addition equations on the construction paper.

2. Help your child read the equations (e.g., $1 + 2 = \_\_$).

3. Let her put the appropriate number of popcorn kernels on or around the numbers in the equation (e.g., the number 1 gets one kernel and the number 2 gets two kernels).

4. Ask her how many kernels she has in total, and have her put the total number of kernels after the equals sign.

5. Now let her glue the kernels in place.

Activity 7: Pin the Nose on the Clown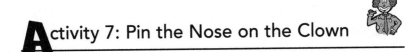

Skills learned: Large motor, memory, letter recognition and phonics (*C*), writing, hand-eye coordination, creativity, colors

Materials: Picture of a clown, red craft pom-pom or cotton ball, tape, a crayon

Instructions:

1. Find or print a coloring page of a clown.

2. Let your child color the picture.

3. Write the word "CLOWN" across the top of the page.

4. Have your child sound out the letter *C*.

5. Let your child practice writing letter *C*s on the coloring page.

6. Tape the picture to the wall at your child's eye level.

7. Let your child feel the paper, and make sure he knows where the nose should be placed.

8. If your child will let you, blindfold him. Otherwise, just have him close his eyes.

9. Put a piece of tape on the pom-pom, and give it to your child.

10. Spin him around a few times, and point him toward the clown. Instruct him to try to put the nose where it should go on the clown. Let him feel his way.

Activity 8: Balloon Experiments

Skills learned: Cause and effect, knowledge of force of air
Materials: Balloon, whistle or party favor blow-out toy
Instructions:

1. Fill the balloon with air, but don't tie it off.

2. Talk about how the air is being held in the balloon. Ask your child what she thinks will happen if you let go of the balloon. Demonstrate by letting go.

3. Fill the balloon again, and show your child what happens when you pull the opening tight to make it just a slit and let the air squeak out slowly. So she doesn't get startled, you may want to warn her that the air will make a loud screeching noise.

4. Fill the balloon again, and explain that you will put the opening of the balloon around the whistle. Ask your child what she thinks

will happen when you let the air out. Demonstrate what happens. Your child will really like this trick and probably will ask you to do it again and again!

5. Fill the balloon again, and give it to your child to conduct her own experiments.

Activity 9: Walk the Tightrope

Skills learned: Large motor, balance, memory, dramatic play
Materials: Masking tape, 2 pipe cleaners
Instructions:

1. Put a 10-foot (3 m) piece of masking tape on your family room floor in a straight line.

2. Explain to your child that he is the tightrope star in the circus.

3. Give him instructions to follow while he balances on the tightrope, such as to walk forward, walk backward, hop on one leg, kick, or walk sideways. Make sure he waves to the crowd!

4. Work his memory by giving him a series of instructions, such as to walk the tightrope going backward and then come back hopping.

5. To really challenge his ability to balance, place a pipe cleaner in the palm of each of his hands and have him walk the tightrope, palms open, without dropping the pipe cleaners. Make sure his arms are outstretched for better balance.

6. For another challenge, place some sugar packets or other small objects on the back of each of his hands and have him walk the tightrope without dropping the objects.

7. Make sure you give him a grand introduction each time he walks the tightrope.

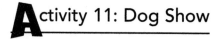ctivity 10: Shadow Matching

Skills learned: Fine motor, object discrimination, matching

Materials: Construction paper, pencil, small animal cutouts (found on the Internet)

Instructions:

1. Trace two of each animal on the construction paper, and shade them in with the pencil.

2. Give the pencil to your child, and have her draw lines to match the pairs of shadows.

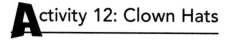ctivity 11: Dog Show

Skills learned: Dramatic play, large motor

Materials: Hula hoop, pillows, graham crackers or other treats (optional)

Instructions:

1. Set up an obstacle course in your family room. Use anything in your house that would make a good obstacle course, such as pillows to sit on and chairs to climb over and through.

2. Let your child pretend to be a dog in the circus as he goes through the obstacle course.

3. If you have a hula hoop, let your child jump through it.

4. Pat his head and tell him, "Good doggie." Consider giving him a graham cracker treat every time he goes through the hoop without touching the sides.

Activity 12: Clown Hats

Skills learned: Following written instructions, counting, fine motor, number recognition

Materials: 2 pieces of construction paper, glue, transparent tape, yarn, hole punch, children's safety scissors, small craft accessories (e.g., pom-poms, sequins, beads)

Instructions:

1. Draw a large circle on one piece of construction paper. Also draw a straight line from the edge of the circle to the center.

2. Help your child cut out the circle. Have her cut the straight line to the center of the circle, too.

3. Make a cone out of the circle, and tape it in place.

4. Make an instruction sheet for your child. The instruction sheet should explain how many of each craft item she should glue onto the hat. For example, if you want her to glue nine sequins, write the number 9 on the instruction sheet and glue a sequin next to it. Make sure you choose numbers your child is currently working on.

5. Give the instruction sheet to your child, and let her follow the instructions.

6. Punch two holes on opposite sides at the bottom of the hat, and string the yarn through to secure the hat to your child's head.

Review Time

- What would happen if I blow up a balloon and let it go without tying it off?
- What do you think elephant skin feels like?
- Can you find the letters *C*, *E*, and *P* in the crafts?
- What sounds do *C* as in *clown* and *E* and in *elephant* make?
- What was your favorite part of the lesson? Mine was . . .

Lesson 22

Wind

Featured Letters: A, C, D, I, K, N, and W

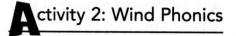 **ntroductory Activity: Wind Book**

Skills learned: Prereading, knowledge of wind, reading comprehension, listening

Instructions:

1. Read aloud a book about wind, and ask your child some comprehension questions.

2. Take this time to discuss what wind is. Ask your child to explain what wind feels like. How can you tell if it's windy if you're inside? What kinds of things blow in the wind?

Activity 2: Wind Phonics

Skills learned: Letter recognition and phonics (*W, I, N, D*)

Materials: White felt, fabric interfacing, or white construction paper; black marker; felt board (optional)

Instructions:

1. Cut four clouds out of the felt, fabric interfacing, or construction paper. Write a different uppercase letter on each cloud to spell out *wind*.

2. Jumble the clouds, and place them on the felt board.

3. Invite your child to the felt board, and explain that you are going to help her spell *wind* with the available letters.

4. Sound out a letter, and ask your child to identify the letter and place it at the top of the board. Do this with each letter until *wind* is spelled out.

Variation:

1. For a greater challenge, make extra clouds with letters not found in the word *wind*. Use letters that look similar, such as *M, L, V,* and *B*.

2. For a lesser challenge, if your child is not quite ready to sound out letters, tell her what letters to find. She will have to identify each letter and place it at the top of the felt board. Make sure you sound out each letter with her as you go along.

Activity 3: Kite Matching

Skills learned: Visual discrimination, memory, logic, color recognition, number recognition, counting

Materials: Various patterned papers, construction paper (various colors), scissors

Instructions:

1. Cut out several kite shapes from the various patterned papers. Cut the kites in half, and mix them up.

2. Give the pile of kite halves to your child, and have her find the matches.

Variation:

1. Hide half of each kite in your family room.

2. Have your child take one of the remaining kite halves and look for its hidden match. If she finds one that doesn't match, she should leave it there and continue looking for the correct match.

Variation:

1. For a different way to do the activity, cut several pairs of kites from various colors of construction paper.

2. Have your child match the pairs of colored kites.

3. For a greater challenge, do this number-matching activity. Take each kite, cut in half down the middle, and write a number on one half and put the matching number of dots on the other half. For example, if you write the number 7 on one half, the other half of the kite should have seven dots.

4. Let your child match the kite halves by counting the dots.

Activity 4: Windy Cloud Writing Practice

Skills learned: Letter recognition and phonics (*W* and *C*), writing, fine motor

Materials: White construction paper, children's safety scissors, pencil

Instructions:

1. Draw the shape of a cloud on the white construction paper. Make two handwriting practice lines across the cloud. Write a sample *W* on one line and a sample *C* on the other line.

2. Have your child cut out the cloud with the safety scissors.

3. Make sure he knows that *C* stands for *cloud* and *W* stands for *wind*, and have him sound out the letters. Then have him practice writing *W*s and *C*s.

Activity 5: Paper Bag Kites

Skills learned: Letter recognition and phonics (*K*), measurement, concept of flight, fine and large motor

Materials: Small paper lunch bag, crepe paper, string, glue, hole punch, hole reinforcements

Instructions:

1. Punch two holes at the top of the bag on opposite sides, and apply hole reinforcements. Cut one piece of string about 3 feet (1 m) long.

2. Have your child sound out the word *kite* with you. Make sure she understands *K* stands for *kite*. Write the letter *K* on one side of the bag.

3. On the other side of the bag, draw handwriting practice lines and a sample letter *K*.

4. Have your child practice writing her letter *K*s on one line.

5. Have her put the string through the holes, and help her tie it off. This is what your child will hold while flying her kite.

6. Have your child measure several pieces of crepe paper to the length of her arm.

7. Let her glue the crepe paper to the bottom of the bag.

8. Explain how a kite flies in the wind. Ask her if she can name other things that fly in the wind (e.g., birds, butterflies, airplanes). Write some of the things she names on the paper bag.

9. Open the paper bag outside, and let her run around to fly her new kite.

Activity 6: Wind Stick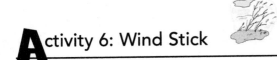

Skills learned: Knowledge of how wind blows objects, fine and large motor

Materials: Glue, water, paintbrush, tissue paper (various colors), scissors, crepe paper, any kind of wooden stick (e.g., small paddle, paint stir stick)

Instructions:

1. Make a glue mixture of 1 tablespoon glue and 2 tablespoons water.

2. Let your child cover the stick with glue.

3. Cut out small squares from the various colors of tissue paper. Give him a handful of squares, and let him put them on the stick.

4. Have your child tear a few long pieces of crepe paper, about the length of his arm.

5. Use full-strength glue to attach the long pieces of crepe paper.

6. Ask your child what he thinks will happen if he runs around with the wind stick. Will the crepe paper remain hanging, or will it fly behind? If it's a windy day, what does he think will happen to the crepe paper if he just stands still?

7. Allow the stick to dry, and let your child run around outside, watching the crepe paper follow behind him.

Activity 7: Paper Airplanes

Skills learned: Logic, knowledge of heavy and light, letter recognition and phonics (A), writing, fine motor

Materials: Printer paper or colored construction paper, pencil or crayon

Instructions:

1. Tell your child A stands for *airplane*. Have her sound out the letter A.

2. Draw a handwriting practice line on a sheet of printer paper, and show your child how to make a letter A. Let her practice writing it on the handwriting practice line.

3. Use printer paper or construction paper to make several paper airplanes with your child. Let her help you fold them. Instructions on how to make a paper airplane can be found on the Internet. You can even find printable patterns.

4. Go outside, and let her experiment with throwing the planes.

5. Ask her what she thinks will happen if you put some leaves or twigs in the center crease of the airplane. Will it still be able to fly? What if something heavier were in the plane, like pennies taped to the wings? Will it stay in the air?

6. Let your child experiment flying the airplane with different small objects attached.

Activity 8: Bubbles Experiment

Skills learned: Logic

Materials: 1 container of bubble solution and a bubble wand

Instructions:

1. You'll want to do this activity on a breezy day.

2. Go to a place inside your house where you don't mind blowing bubbles (e.g., bathroom, laundry room, garage). Make sure you temporarily turn off your heating or air-conditioning system so it doesn't interfere with this experiment.

3. Ask your child what he thinks will happen when you blow bubbles where there is no wind. Will they fly up in the air, or will they drop to the ground?

4. Let him try blowing some bubbles, too.

5. Go outside and ask him the same questions. Let him blow bubbles to see what happens.

Activity 9: Feather Game

Skills learned: Large motor

Materials: 1 small feather or a 1-inch (2.5 cm) square piece of tissue paper

Instructions:

1. Give her the feather or square of tissue paper, and have her try and keep it in the air by blowing on it.

2. Then try blowing together, and see how long you can keep it flying!

Activity 10: Windy Relay Race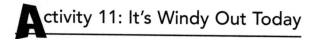

Skills learned: Large motor

Materials: Masking tape, tissue paper

Instructions:

1. Use the masking tape to outline an obstacle course in your family room.

2. Make a small ball out of a small piece of tissue paper.

3. Give the ball to your child, and let him try to blow the ball through the obstacle course as fast as he can. Make sure he doesn't use his hands!

Activity 11: It's Windy Out Today

Skills learned: Rhythm, rhyming, dramatic play

Materials: Leaf cutouts

Instructions:

1. Cut out some leaves from construction paper, or gather some real leaves.

2. Sing the following song with your child, and have your child act out each verse:

It's Windy Out Today (to the tune of "The Farmer in the Dell")
It's windy out today, it's windy out today,
High-ho the merry-o, it's windy out today.

It's blowing all the leaves, it's blowing all the leaves, (Throw the
leaf cutouts up in the air.)
High-ho the merry-o, it's blowing all the leaves.

It's moving all the trees, it's moving all the trees, (Pretend to be
a tree rocking gently back and forth.)
High-ho the merry-o, it's moving all the trees.

Birds fly in the breeze, birds fly in the breeze, (Pretend to be a
bird flying.)
High-ho the merry-o, birds fly in the breeze.

The pollen makes me sneeze, the pollen makes me sneeze, (Pretend to sneeze.)
High-ho the merry-o, the pollen makes me sneeze. (Pretend to
sneeze.)

It's windy out today, it's windy out today,
High-ho the merry-o, it's windy out today.

Review Time

- Can you name some things that the wind blows?
- Can you find the letters *A*, *C*, *K*, and *W* in our crafts?
- How can you tell it is windy if you are inside?
- What sounds do *C* as in *cloud*, *K* as in *kite*, and *W* as in *wind* make?
- What was your favorite part of the lesson? Mine was . . .

Lesson 23

ABCDEFGHIJKLMNOPQRSTUVWXYZ

Spring Rain

Featured Letters: A, I, N, R, and U

Introductory Activity: Rain Book

Skills learned: Prereading, listening, knowledge of rain, reading comprehension

Instructions:

1. Read aloud any informative rain book (at your child's level) to your child, and discuss what signs of rain can be seen (e.g., puddles, mud, rainbow). Ask your child comprehension questions about the story you read.

2. If your child is ready, discuss the rain cycle. Heat causes water to spread out and evaporate, or rise into air. It is cooler up in the sky, so the evaporated water begins to "huddle" together and forms drops, which form clouds. When the clouds get heavy with water, the rain comes down and the cycle begins again.

Activity 2: Umbrella Poem

Skills learned: Colors, rhyming, counting backward, subtraction
Materials: Red, blue, green, yellow, purple felt or fabric interfacing and crayons; scissors; construction paper; felt board
Instructions:

1. Cut out an umbrella template from the construction paper. Pin the template onto a felt piece. Trace the template, and cut out the felt umbrella. Repeat for each piece of felt. If using interfacing, trace 5 umbrellas onto the interfacing using the template. Color the umbrellas red, blue, green, yellow, and purple. Cut them out.

2. Put the umbrellas on the felt board, and recite the following poem. Have your child remove the umbrellas when prompted in the poem. Emphasize the number of remaining umbrellas as you subtract.

Five Umbrellas

One, two, three, four, five umbrellas sitting by the door,
Father grabs the red one, and now there are four. (Remove red.)
Four bright umbrellas now long for rain to see,
Brother grabs the blue one, and then there are three. (Remove blue.)
Three umbrellas hope the sky will not turn blue,
Sister grabs the yellow one, and now there are two. (Remove yellow.)
Two umbrellas cry, "We want to have some fun."
Baby grabs the purple one, and now there is one. (Remove purple.)
One lone umbrella says, "Oh, now what will I do?"
But Mother grabs the green one and it goes outside, too. (Remove green.)

Activity 3: Umbrella Math

Skills learned: Addition and subtraction, counting
Materials: Construction paper, scissors, marker
Instructions:
1. Draw seven umbrellas and seven childlike figures on the construction paper, and cut them out.
2. Show your child three figures and two umbrellas. Tell your child that it is starting to rain and the kids need umbrellas. Have your child distribute the two umbrellas to two of the kids. Are there enough umbrellas? How many more does she need?
3. Continue this activity with different combinations: for example, five umbrellas and two kids (three extra umbrellas), or six kids and two umbrellas (four more umbrellas are needed).

Activity 4: Rainy Day Rhythm

Skills learned: Fine and large motor; listening; rhyming; knowledge of soft and loud, fast and slow
Instructions:
Recite the following poem, and have your child follow your motions.

Rain Is Falling All Around
Rain is falling all around, making puddles on the ground. (Slap hands on the table.)
Rain is pounding on our roof. I hope that it is waterproof. (Pound fists on table.)
Oh! I hear the thunder clap. Can you make a sound like that? (Clap hands loudly.)
As the rain is slowing down, I hear its pitter-patter sound, (Slowly slap hands on table.)

Softly now but falling still. I'm watching from my windowsill.

(Softly pat hands on table.)

Now it stops, and I can grin. The world is fresh and clean again!

(Give a big smile.)

Activity 5: Evaporation Paintings

Skills learned: Knowledge of evaporation, fine motor

Materials: Water, cup, large paintbrush, hot sidewalk

Instructions:

1. On a hot and sunny day, give your child water and a paintbrush. Have her dip her paintbrush into the water and paint a simple picture on a sunny patch of sidewalk. Have her write her name, too.

2. Watch the painting disappear because the heat causes the water to evaporate.

Activity 6: Absorption Chart

Skills learned: Knowledge of absorbent materials, fine motor

Materials: Large poster board, construction paper, black marker, test materials (sponge, paper towel, coin, towel, cork, wood chip, foil, wax paper), eyedropper, glue

Instructions:

1. Create the following chart on poster board. Using construction paper, create a label for each item that is being tested.

Does It Absorb Water?

Yes	*No*

2. Using the eyedropper and water, have your child see which items absorb water.

3. Tell him the beginning letter for each object, and have him find its label. Have him glue the labels under Yes or No columns on the chart.

4. Discuss why he thinks some items absorb water while others don't.

Activity 7: Rain Stick

Skills learned: Fine motor, creativity, writing, letter recognition and phonics (R, A, I, N)

Materials: Paper-towel or wrapping-paper tubes, coffee stir sticks (thin straws) cut into 1½ inch (3.5 cm) pieces, popcorn kernels and dry rice, electrical tape, decorations of choice, construction paper, glue, 1 nail

Instructions:

1. Cover one opening of the tube with construction paper and tape. Use the nail to poke holes all along the tube. The holes need to be spread all around the tube—the more the better.

2. Help your child insert the cut-up stir sticks into the holes you made in the tube. Allow the end of each stir-stick to barely show. You don't want the stir sticks to fall into the tube.

3. Wrap electrical tape all around the tube to secure the stir sticks.

4. Have your child pour popcorn and rice into the open end of the tube. The amount depends on the sound you want your rain stick to make.

5. Cover the open end of the tube with construction paper and tape.

6. Have your child cover the entire tube with construction paper.

7. Have her write *rain* on the rain stick or decorate it with *R*s.

8. Flip the rain stick up and down to hear the "rain" fall.

Activity 8: Rain Art

Skills learned: Fine motor, colors

Materials: Construction paper (1 brightly colored and 1 light blue or white), blue glitter glue or white glue tinted with blue food coloring, black permanent marker, toothpick, cotton-tip applicators, glue, cotton balls, gray washable paint, aluminum foil, children's safety scissors

Instructions:

1. Draw a half circle about 3 inches (7.5 cm) high on a piece of colorful construction paper. Draw several small puddles on the aluminum foil.

2. Give your child a piece of light blue or white construction paper.

3. Have your child cut out the half circle you drew and glue it in the center of the light blue or white piece of construction paper to make the top of an umbrella. Have her glue on the toothpick to make a handle for the umbrella.

4. Help your child cut out the aluminum puddles and glue them to the bottom of her paper.

5. Give your child the cotton-tip applicator, and have her dip it in the glitter glue or tinted glue. Let her use the applicator and glue to drop "raindrops" all over her paper. The goal here is not to spread or smear the glue but to gently drop it with controlled movements.

6. Let your child manipulate the cotton balls to spread them out. She can brush these with gray paint and then glue them on her rain picture to make clouds.

Activity 9: Cloud Counting

Skills learned: Number recognition, matching, counting

Materials: White construction paper or fabric interfacing, scissors, glue, crayons or markers, extra sheet of construction paper

Instructions:

1. Draw clouds on the construction paper or fabric interfacing. Divide the clouds into two equal groups. On one group, write a different number on each cloud. On the other group, draw raindrops on each cloud to match the numbers in the other set. (You and not your child should cut these clouds out.)

2. Have your child match the number clouds to the raindrop clouds.

3. Glue the clouds on another piece of construction paper, or save them in a sandwich bag to do again later.

Activity 10: Rain Puddle Toss

Skills learned: Large motor; knowledge of small, medium, and large; ordering; hand–eye coordination

Materials: Brown paper grocery bags or brown construction paper, scissors, beanbag

Instructions:

1. Cut out small, medium, and large rain puddles from the brown paper.

2. Spread the puddles out on the floor, and give your child the beanbag. Ask him to throw the beanbag onto the largest puddle, smallest puddle, and so on. Mix the puddles up, and try again.

Variation:

1. For a greater challenge, write letters or numbers on the puddles.

2. Have your child throw the beanbag on a puddle with a specific letter or number.

Activity 11: Puddle Jump

Skills learned: Large motor; listening; recognition of letters, numbers, colors, or shapes

Materials: Brown paper grocery bags, music, music player, masking tape

Instructions:

1. Cut out puddle shapes from the paper bags, and tape them on your floor in a circle.

2. Draw or write a different shape, number, letter, or color on each puddle.

3. Have your child stand on a puddle. Start the music and have her hop from puddle to puddle. Tell her that when the music stops, she must stop on the puddle she is on. If she names the object on her puddle she stays in the game. If you don't want to use elimination, tell your child what she is standing on when she misses and play again. This game can also be played with several children.

Activity 12: Wet Chalk Art

Skills learned: Large and fine motor, letter recognition and phonics (*R*, *U*), name recognition, creativity, writing, colors

Materials: Outside chalk, water

Instructions:

1. Take your child outside, and hose down the driveway. Give him the outside chalk, and let him draw on the driveway. Point out the vibrant colors.

2. Have him practice writing his name, *R* for *rain*, and *U* for *umbrella*.

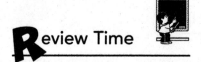 **R**eview Time

- Where does rain come from?
- Can you find the letters *R* and *U* in our activities?
- Where did the water on the sidewalk go?
- What sounds do *R* as in *rain* and *U* as in *umbrella* make?
- What was your favorite activity in this lesson? Mine was . . .

A B C D E F G H I J K L M N O P Q R S T U V W X Y Z

Garden

Featured Letters: F, G, and V

Introductory Activity: Garden Book

Skills learned: Prereading, familiarity with a garden, rhythm, reading comprehension, listening

Instructions:

1. Read aloud a garden book, and ask some comprehension questions.

2. Discuss what might be found in a garden. Also use this time to talk about what plants and flowers need to grow (e.g., sunlight, water, soil). You may also want to discuss the different animals and bugs that live in a garden.

3. Sing the following song to help your child remember three important things a plant needs to grow. Make sure to sing it several times, and encourage your child to sing with you.

Soil, Water, and Sun (to the tune of "The Farmer in the Dell")
Soil, water, and sun,
Soil, water, and sun,

It takes all three to grow a seed,
Soil, water, and sun.

Activity 2: Color by Number

Skills learned: Familiarity with flower parts, following instructions, fine motor, letter recognition and phonics (*G*)

Materials: Coloring page of a flower, crayons or color pencils

Instructions:

1. Use a number system to make a coloring guide and label the flower on the coloring page. For example, instead of using the word *green*, you should write "1 = (color a small circle of green)" on your coloring guide and mark the spots that should be colored green on the coloring page with 1s. Then your child knows all the 1s are green, all the 2s are a different color, and so on.

2. Point out the different parts of a flower on the coloring page (e.g., roots, stem, leaves, petals, stamen). You may have to draw in some roots.

3. Have your child color by number.

4. When she is finished coloring, have her help you label the different parts.

5. You may want to take this time to discuss what a flower needs to grow.

6. Write "__ ARDEN" across the top of the page, and have her tell you what letter is at the beginning of *garden*. Make sure you sound it out, and have your child sound it out, too.

Activity 3: Hand Flower

Skills learned: Letter recognition and phonics (*F*), fine motor, writing

Materials: 2 pieces of construction paper, muffin cup, children's safety scissors, glue, pencil, craft stick (or chenille stem)

Instructions:

1. Let your child trace his hand on a piece of construction paper with a pencil. Some kids trace without a problem, but others may find it difficult. Make sure to give him a helping hand if it gets too frustrating.

2. Cut out the hand.

3. Give the muffin cup to your child. Let him flatten it out and glue the bottom of it to the palm of his paper hand.

4. Let him cut the edges of the muffin cup to make a fringe.

5. Give him the pencil, and let him wrap the "petals" (fingers and fringe) around the pencil to make them curl.

6. Have him color or paint the craft stick green, and glue it to another piece of construction paper.

7. Next, have him glue the flower to the top of the stem.

8. Write "FLOWER" at the top of the page, and let him practice making the letter *F*. Make sure he understands what the letter *F* sounds like.

Activity 4: Colored Flowers Experiment

Skills learned: Knowledge of how to make different colors, logic, creativity

Materials: Food coloring (primary colors); white daisies or carnations; 4 cups, each filled one-third with water

Instructions:

1. Ask your child to help you color the water in each cup. Tell her you're making colors that don't come in a standard pack of food coloring so she can see what colors you need to mix to make purple, green, or orange. Use yellow and blue to make green, red and yellow to make orange, and blue and red to make purple.

2. Show her the white flowers, and ask her what she thinks will happen when she dips the flowers in the colored water.

3. Let her experiment by dipping the flowers into the colored water.

Variation:

1. Color the water with the primary colors that come in the food-coloring pack.

2. Let your child dip a flower in red and yellow to make an orange flower, or red and blue to make a purple one, and so on.

3. Put the stem of a white flower into colored water. (You may need to let them soak for several minutes.)

4. Ask your child what she thinks will happen to the flower as it drinks up the water.

5. Let the flower sit for a day or two. You will notice the flower petals begin to change color.

Activity 5: Homemade Vase Collage

Skills learned: Letter recognition and phonics (*V*), writing, sorting, shapes, color recognition

Materials: Milk carton, scissors, construction paper (4 different colors), glue, crayon

Instructions:

1. Cut off the top of the milk carton. Cut out circles, squares, rectangles, and ovals from the construction paper. Make sure you cut several of each shape and use each of the colors.

2. Give the shapes to your child. First have him sort all the shapes by color. Then have him sort them by shape.

3. Tell your child that he will decorate a vase. Make sure he knows that *V* stands for *vase* and have him sound out the letter *V*.

4. Let your child decide if he would like to decorate each side of the vase with matching colors or matching shapes. Either way, each side of the vase should be covered with matching shapes or matching colors.

5. After the vase dries, let your child practice writing *V*s on the vase with the crayon.

Activity 6: Vase Race

Skills learned: Letter and number recognition, following instructions, large motor, memory

Materials: Vase (use the one from Activity 5 or a plastic cup), craft sticks, construction paper (various colors), marker

Instructions:

1. Make flowers from the construction paper, and glue them to the craft sticks.

2. Write a number or letter in the middle of each flower. Make sure the numbers are ones that your child is currently working on. Place the flowers in a nonbreakable vase.

3. On a piece of paper, write the numbers and letters you used in a column, and draw a box next to each so your child can check them off.

4. Give the sheet of paper to your child, and have her start with the letter or number at the top of the list. Leaving the sheet of paper behind, have her race across the room to the vase, identify the letter or number on a flower, race back, and mark an *X* in the box. She'll repeat this process until she has found all of the flowers.

Variation:

1. For a greater challenge, include flowers with additional numbers and letters that are not listed on the sheet.

2. Instead of using a vase, hide the flowers around your family room or backyard. Then your child will need to find the appropriate flower before bringing it back to mark off the sheet.

Activity 7: Vase Comparison

Skills learned: Colors; counting; number recognition; knowledge of more and less, same and different; visual discrimination; matching

Materials: Construction paper, color pencils

Instructions:

1. Draw four vases according to the following directions. Color the vases so that two are the same color, and the other two are different colors—for example, color two blue vases, a red vase, and a green vase. Also, draw the vases so that two are the same size and the other two are different sizes—for example, draw a small vase, a large vase, and two medium-sized vases. Finally, draw a different number of flowers in each vase.

2. Have your child identify the two vases that are the same size. Next, have your child identify the two vases with the matching color.

3. Let your child count the number of flowers in each vase.

4. After your child counts the flowers in a vase, write the number of flowers on the vase. Make sure you show him the number after you write it.

5. Point to two vases, and have your child identify which vase has the most flowers. Point to two more vases, and have your child identify which has the fewest flowers.

6. Have your child identify the biggest vase, smallest vase, and the two of equal size.

7. Ask your child to identify specific numbers written on the vases. For example, if there is a vase with the number 7, ask him to point to it.

8. Encourage your child to discuss all the things that are the same and different about the vases and flowers.

Activity 8: Plants Need Sunlight

Skills learned: Knowledge of planting and what a seed needs to grow

Materials: Lima beans, clear plastic cups, soil, water, a window ledge that gets sun, and a dark shelf or closet

Instructions:

1. Before beginning, discuss what it takes for a plant to grow (e.g., water, soil, sunlight).

2. Have your child fill the cups halfway with soil.

3. Let your child put a couple of lima beans in each cup. Make sure they are placed in the soil and next to the side of the cup so the beans are visible.

4. Add about another inch of soil, and let your child sprinkle it with water.

5. Put one cup in a place where it will get plenty of sunlight and the other in a dark place, like a closet or cabinet.

6. Ask your child what she thinks will happen to the bean seeds in the sunlight and what will happen to the bean seeds in the cabinet.

7. Have your child check on the seeds every day for progress, and sprinkle them with water if needed.

8. Discuss with your child the differences in each plant, and explore why they are different.

9. After your child has had a chance to observe what occurred to the bean seed in the cabinet, place it in the sun and watch it grow!

Activity 9: Flower Parts Puzzle

Skills learned: Familiarity with the different parts of a flower, logic, letter recognition and phonics (*F*)

Materials: Flower coloring page, color pencils or crayons, glue, construction paper

Instructions:

1. Cut out and color a large flower from a flower coloring page.

2. Cut the flower into pieces: leaves, stalk, flower, and roots (you may have to draw your own roots).

3. Give the parts to your child, and have him put them together and glue them on the construction paper.

4. Explain each part of the flower, and write the names next to each flower part: petal, stamen, carpel, stalk, leaf, roots.

5. Write the word "FLOWER" across the top of the construction paper, and have him sound out the letter *F* with you.

Activity 10: Vegetable Painting

Skills learned: Patterns, letter recognition and phonics (*V*), fine motor

Materials: Construction paper, vegetables (e.g., cucumber, zucchini, broccoli), paint

Instructions:

1. Cut the various vegetables into small pieces that your child can use for stamping.

2. Write a large letter *V* on the construction paper.

3. Make sure your child knows that *V* stands for *vegetable*, and have her sound out the letter *V*.

4. Ask your child to name all the vegetables she can think of. Help her list some if she can't. Ask her to tell you her favorite vegetable.

5. Give the various vegetables to your child. Identify the vegetables that she doesn't recognize.

6. Let your child stamp a pattern on the letter *V* with the vegetable stamps.

Activity 11: Garden Caterpillar

Skills learned: Colors, sorting, fine motor, matching

Materials: Craft pom-poms (various colors); construction paper; color pens, pencils, or crayons; glue; google eyes

Instructions:

1. Use the color pens to draw medium-sized circles on the construction paper in the shape of a caterpillar. Each circle should be a different color.

2. Encourage your child to discuss the different bugs he might find in a garden.

3. Give the craft pom-poms to your child, and have him sort them according to color.

4. Let him glue the colored pom-poms onto the caterpillar. Make sure your child matches the pom-poms to the correct colored circle on the caterpillar (e.g., all the green pom-poms go in the green circle, red pom-poms in the red circle).

5. Let your child glue on the google eyes.

Review Time

- What happens to white flowers when they are dipped in colored water?
- What three things does a seed need to grow?
- Can you find the letters *F*, *G*, and *V* in the activities?
- What sounds do *G* as in *garden* and *V* as in *vegetable* make?
- Where are the roots of a plant?
- What was your favorite part of the lesson? Mine was . . .

Lesson 25

A B C D E F G H I J K L M N O P Q R S T U V W X Y Z

Savanna

Featured Letters: A and Z

Introductory Activity: Savanna Book

Skills learned: Prereading, knowledge of African animals and their environment, listening, reading comprehension

Instructions:

1. Read aloud a book about the savanna, and ask your child some comprehension questions.

2. Use a global map to show your child where Africa is located.

Activity 2: A Is for *Africa*

Skills learned: Letter recognition and phonics (*A*), prewriting

Materials: Construction paper, pencil or crayon

Instructions:

1. At the top of the construction paper, write an uppercase *A* and a lowercase *a*. Randomly write other uppercase and lowercase *A*s, *V*s, *H*s, and *G*s all over the construction paper.

2. Make sure your child knows that *A* stands for *Africa*, and have him sound out the letter *A*.

3. Show him the top of the construction paper, and make sure he knows what uppercase and lowercase *A*s look like.

4. Give your child the pencil or crayon, and have him circle all of the letter *A*s on the page.

Activity 3: Monkey See, Monkey Do

Skills learned: Large motor

Instructions:

1. Sit facing your child.

2. Have your child make movements with her hands. As she does so, mirror her movements.

3. Have your child mirror the movements you make, too.

Activity 4: Zebra Stripes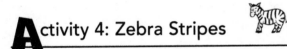

Skills learned: Letter recognition and phonics (*Z*), fine motor, colors, knowledge of zebras, counting, writing

Materials: White construction paper, children's safety scissors, black tempura paint, cotton-tip applicator (or fine paintbrush)

Instructions:

1. Cut out the shape of a zebra from the white construction paper.

2. Cut out a mane and a tail from the black construction paper.

3. Give the zebra to your child, and let him paint the stripes with a cotton-tip applicator or fine paintbrush.

4. Let your child use the safety scissors to fringe the mane and tail.

5. After the paint has dried on the zebra, have your child glue the mane and tail at the appropriate places.

6. Make sure your child knows that *zebra* starts with the letter *Z*. Have him say the word and sound out the letter.

7. If your child is already familiar with the letter *Z*, then say the word *zebra* and ask him what letter it starts with.

8. Draw a handwriting practice line on the paper and a sample *Z*. Have your child practice writing his letter *Z*s.

Variation:

For a greater challenge, instruct your child to paint a certain number of stripes on the zebra for the body and each leg. Choose numbers you are currently working on with your child. For example, have him paint twelve stripes on the zebra's body, six stripes on one leg, and nine stripes on another leg.

Activity 5: Animal Movements

Skills learned: Large motor, dramatic play, imagination

Materials: Pictures of savanna animals

Instructions:

1. Place all the animal pictures facedown.

2. Let your child pick an animal picture. Then have her act out how that animal would move while you guess the animal she is pretending to be.

3. Make sure she understands that she is to act out only the movements—not the animal noises.

4. Take turns acting and guessing.

Activity 6: Spiral Snakes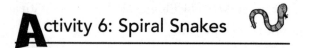

Skills learned: Fine motor

Materials: Green tempera paint, white construction paper, children's safety scissors, google eyes, black marker, yarn, hole punch

Instructions:

1. Cut out a circle about 9 inches (23 cm) in diameter from the white construction paper.

2. Have your child use his thumb and green paint to stamp thumbprints on the front and the back of the paper until it is well-covered.

3. After the paper has dried, use the black marker to draw a spiral on the paper, stopping 4 inches (10 cm) from the center of the circle. The center will be the snake's head.

4. Have your child carefully cut on the line.

5. Glue on the google eyes or use the marker to make eyes on the head of the snake.

6. Punch a hole through the head of the snake, and have your child thread the yarn through.

7. Tie the yarn so it won't slip back through the hole.

Activity 7: Safari Hat

Skills learned: Fine motor, creativity

Materials: Newspaper, clear packing tape, safari stickers or animal stamps

Instructions:

1. Lay out one large piece of newspaper.

2. Let your child decorate the center of the newspaper with stickers or stamps.

3. Put the center of the newspaper on your child's head. Wrap a piece of clear packing tape on the newspaper around her head.

4. Let her help you curl the edges up and crumple as you go.

5. She's ready for a safari!

Activity 8: Safari Map

Skills learned: Reading a map

Materials: Paper bag, black or brown crayon, hidden treasure

Instructions:

1. Crumple and uncrumple a paper bag several times until it has a soft, worn feel to it.

2. Draw a map of your yard or your home on the paper bag. Draw a dotted line indicating the path to find the hidden treasure. Along the dotted line, mark three places in the yard where you would like your child to stop for clues.

3. Cut the bag into four pieces. Each piece should show the dotted line going to the next clue.

4. Place the first piece of the map at the start of the treasure hunt. It should have a dotted line showing your child where to go for the second clue. The second clue should be hidden where the map indicates and should show where to find the third clue. The third clue also should be hidden where the map indicates and should show where to find the fourth clue. Finally, the fourth clue should be hidden where the map indicates and should show where to find the hidden treasure.

5. The treasure could be a tasty treat or maybe some trinkets you picked up at the dollar store.

6. Let your child wear the hat he made in Activity 7 of this lesson.

Activity 9: What's Hiding in the Grass?

Skills learned: Prewriting, fine motor, logic, knowledge of savanna animals

Materials: Printer paper, card stock, scissors, yellow and brown crayons

Instructions:

1. Print a coloring page of a savanna animal on the card stock. Cut out the animal.

2. Give the printer paper and yellow crayon to your child, and have him cover the entire page with yellow grass as is found in the savanna.

3. Have your child cover his eyes while you slip an animal cutout under the paper grassland. Tape both pieces of paper to a hard surface so they stay in place.

4. Tell your child that an animal is hiding in the grassland, and give him clues about what kind of animal it is. For example, if it is an elephant, tell him it is a very large animal with a long trunk for a nose.

5. After he has guessed the animal, let him check to see if he is correct by gently rubbing the side of the brown crayon (with the crayon paper removed) over the printer paper to reveal what is hiding. The outline of the animal will appear.

6. Repeat these steps if you would like him to guess more than one animal.

Activity 10: Giraffes Are Tall!

Skills learned: Comparison, measurement, counting, knowledge of giraffes

Materials: String or yarn, tape measure, chalk

Instructions:

1. Encourage your child to discuss giraffes. Are they tall? What do they eat? (*leaves*) How do they reach the leaves?

2. Explain that giraffes can be up to 17 feet (5 m) tall. Their legs can be 6 feet (2 m) long and help them run up to 35 miles per hour (65 km/h).

3. Go outside and explain that he will be measuring 6 feet (2 m) by using the tape measure. Have your child walk with the tape measure and count out 6 feet (2 m) while you hold it in place.

4. Hold the tape measure in place while your child uses chalk to draw a 6-foot line (2 m) along the tape measure.

5. Ask your child if he thinks the line he measured is taller or shorter than he is. Have him guess how tall he is.

6. Have your child lie down next to the chalk line with his feet at one end. Draw an outline of his body with the chalk. By comparing his outline with the 6-foot (2 m) chalk line, have him compare his height to the length of the giraffe legs.

7. Get the tape measure out, and let your child measure the height of his chalk outline.

8. Encourage your child to compare the differences.

Variation:

For additional comparison, measure 17 feet (5 m) so your child can compare the overall height of the giraffe to the length of giraffe legs and the height of the chalk outline of your child. Make sure he helps you measure by counting out the feet (or meters) as you go.

Activity 11: Thirsty Giraffe

Skills learned: Knowledge of giraffes, large motor

Materials: Aluminum pie pan, water

Instructions:

1. Explain that giraffes can live without water for a month. Giraffes can be up to 17 feet (5 m) tall. So in order for a giraffe to drink water, it has to spread its long legs wide enough to reach water.

2. Put a small amount of water in the pie pan. Have your child put her hands and feet on the floor on either side of the pan. Ask her to try and take a drink of water without bending her elbows or knees. She'll have to spread her arms and legs enough so her mouth can reach the water.

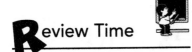

Review Time

- Can you name some animals in the savanna?
- What colors are zebras?
- Are giraffes tall or short?
- Are you bigger than a giraffe or smaller?
- Can you find the letters *A* and *Z* in our crafts?
- What sounds do *A* as in *Africa* and *Z* as in *zebra* make?
- What was your favorite part of the lesson? Mine was . . .

Lesson 26

A B C D E F G H I J K L M N O P Q R S T U V W X Y Z

Butterflies and Caterpillars

Featured Letters: B and C

Introductory Activity: Butterfly Book

Skills learned: Prereading, listening, knowledge of butterflies and caterpillars, reading comprehension

Instructions:

Read aloud the butterfly book, and emphasize the life cycle of the butterfly: egg, caterpillar, chrysalis, and butterfly. Ask her questions about the story to check her comprehension.

Activity 2: Butterfly Life-Cycle Model

Skills learned: Knowledge of butterfly symmetry and life cycle, fine motor, listening, creativity, colors, ordinal numbers

Materials: Plastic egg, fabric or felt, small- to medium-sized pompoms, google eyes, glue, 1 old-fashioned clothespin (no spring; found in craft stores), black paint, paintbrush, tissue paper, black chenille stick cut in half, paper-towel tube (painting it green or white is optional)

Instructions:

1. Paint the clothespin black. Cut a 1-by-5-inch strip from the felt or fabric. Cut several 6-by-3-inch (15 by 7.5 cm) rectangles out of the tissue paper.

2. Discuss the butterfly's life cycle: egg, caterpillar, chrysalis, and butterfly.

3. For the caterpillar: Help your child put glue on the fabric strip. Using ordinal numbers, ask her to pick up the pom-poms in a particular order (e.g., the black pom-pom *first*, the red pom-pom *second*) and glue them on the fabric strip. Let dry.

4. For the butterfly: Discuss how the left side of a butterfly matches the right side and this is called symmetry. Have your child pick up one of the tissue-paper rectangles and stuff it lengthwise into the opening of the old-fashioned clothespin. Be sure the tissue paper is centered. Repeat with the other tissue-paper rectangles. Help her wrap half a chenille stick around the top of the clothespin to form antennae.

5. Place the caterpillar in the plastic egg and the butterfly in one end of the paper-towel tube. Discuss the butterfly life cycle with the following steps.

6. Have your child "hatch" the caterpillar from the egg.

7. Let her make the caterpillar crawl around and climb in the empty end of the tube, which is the chrysalis.

8. Let the chrysalis sit for a moment; then have your child "hatch" the butterfly by pulling it from the other end of the tube.

Activity 3: Butterfly Melt

Skills learned: Colors, fine motor, creativity, knowledge of heat

Materials: Wax paper, old crayons without wrappers, handheld pencil sharpener, iron (for adult use only), scissors, marker, hole punch, yarn, construction paper, old newspaper

Instructions:

1. Cut an 8-to-10-inch (20 to 25 cm) butterfly template from construction paper.

2. Have your child sharpen a number of crayons and save the shavings. Let your child identify each color she is shaving. This takes some time so the parent may want to preshave most of the crayons.

3. Have her sprinkle the shavings into the center of a large rectangle of wax paper (wax side up). Lay another same-size piece of wax paper over the shavings (wax side down).

4. Place the wax paper sandwich between layers of newspaper and move to the ironing board.

5. Turn on your iron to the lowest setting possible and iron the wax-paper sandwich to melt the crayons. You can let your child observe from a safe distance, but do not let her participate in this step.

6. When the wax paper cools, have your child lay the butterfly template on the wax-paper sandwich and trace it with a marker.

7. Have her cut out the butterfly shape from the wax paper.

8. Help her punch the top and thread it with yarn to hang.

Activity 4: Power-Packed Activity

Skills learned: Ordering, numbers, fine motor, matching, letter recognition and phonics (B, C), writing

Materials: Construction paper, crayons or markers, scissors, glue, large manila paper

Instructions:

1. Cut five 2-inch (5 cm) diameter construction-paper circles. Write a series of consecutive numbers of your choice on the circles (e.g., 1 to 5, 11 to 15).

2. Cut between five and eight butterfly shapes (3 to 4 inches [7.5 to 9 cm] wide). On the right wing of each butterfly, write a letter. On the left wing of each butterfly, draw a picture that begins with the letter from the right side. For example, write a letter A on the right side and draw an apple on the left. Cut the butterflies in half, and glue all the left wings to the manila paper.

3. Give your child the numbered circles, and have her put them in consecutive order.

4. Help her glue the consecutive circles to the manila paper so they look like a caterpillar. She can add eyes and feet with a crayon.

5. Now have her match the right wings of the butterflies to the left wings, and glue them down.

6. Ask your child what *caterpillar* starts with, and help her write several *C*s underneath her caterpillar. Repeat with *butterfly* and *B*s.

Activity 5: Butterfly Division

Skills learned: Division, counting, knowledge of symmetry, fine motor

Materials: Construction paper (white and other), scissors, black crayon, washable glue

Instructions:

1. On the white construction paper, draw five plain, medium-sized butterflies. Under each butterfly, write a different even number: 2, 4, 6, 8, and 10.

2. Cut out thirty small, identically sized squares from one piece of construction paper.

3. Give your child the butterfly page and pile of squares. Point to the first butterfly and ask her to tell you the number under the butterfly. Have her count out that number of colored squares.

4. Discuss the butterfly's symmetry. The wings on a butterfly look exactly alike, so each wing needs the same number of squares.

5. Have her distribute the squares equally on the butterfly's wings. For example, say her butterfly has four squares. How can she arrange the squares on the butterfly's wings so that each wing will have the same number of squares? Help her conclude that each wing needs two squares. A butterfly with six squares would need three squares on each wing. Continue in this way with all the butterflies.

Activity 6: Gummy-Worm Match

Skills learned: Numbers, colors, prediction, matching, counting
Materials: 36 gummy worms, 4 jars of equal sizes
Instructions:
1. Fill three jars with gummy worms: the first jar with 4 worms, the second with 8 worms, and the third with 12 worms.
2. Fill a fourth jar with a matching amount of 12.
3. Give your child the fourth jar with 12 worms, and have her find the matching jar among the other 3.

Activity 7: Caterpillar Patterns

Skills learned: Fine and large motor, patterning, colors
Materials: Medium raw potatoes, knife, washable paint (3 colors), large manila paper, small paper plates, crayon
Instructions:
1. Cut one or two potatoes in half through the middle. Prepare your paint by pouring 3 colors into their own paper plates.
2. Using the cut end of the potatoes as stamps, begin making some caterpillars out of stamped circles. The circles should create a color pattern—for example, green, green, red, green, green, red. Start two to four different caterpillars with different patterns.

3. Have your child use the potato stamps to continue the patterns you started.

4. You could also have your child create her own caterpillar pattern.

Activity 8: Butterfly Catch

Skills learned: Large motor, hand-eye coordination
Materials: Tissue paper, nets or bowls
Instructions:
1. Cut 30 3-inch (7.5 cm) squares from the tissue paper. Make ten to twenty butterflies out of tissue-paper squares by twisting the paper square in the middle.
2. Throw the butterflies into the air, and have your child run underneath and catch as many as possible with a net or bowl.

Activity 9: Color by Number or Letter

Skills learned: Fine motor, number or letter recognition, colors
Materials: White paper, crayons
Instructions:
1. Draw a simple butterfly on the white paper. Draw a pattern using shapes on one wing, and write a different letter or number in each shape on that wing. Mirror this design on the other wing. On paper, create a key for your letter or number choices by assigning each letter or number a color (e.g., 3 = blue). Write 3 and color a blue square next to it.
2. Have your child color the color by number (or letter) butterfly by using the key.

Activity 10: I Am a Chrysalis

Skills learned: Large motor, dramatic play, knowledge of butterflies
Materials: Roll of toilet paper
Instructions:

1. Tell your child that she is going to pretend to be a chrysalis.
2. Have her stand while you wrap the toilet paper around her to make a chrysalis. Be sure that you don't cover her nose.
3. Tell your child that she is becoming a butterfly inside the chrysalis and that when it is ready, she should burst out of the cocoon. Have her break free and then fly around the room flapping her arms like they are wings.

Activity 11: Life-Cycle Movements with Song

Skills learned: Large motor, knowledge of butterfly's life cycle, rhythm
Instructions:

1. Sing the following song with your child. You and your child should act out each verse.

> *Once I Was (to the tune of "Mary Had a Little Lamb")*
> Once I was a tiny egg, tiny egg, tiny egg. (Child is in fetal position.)
> Once I was a tiny egg, sitting on a leaf.
>
> I popped out as a caterpillar, caterpillar, caterpillar. (Child inches across the floor.)
> I popped out as a caterpillar, inching along the ground.
>
> I grew very tired, very tired, very tired. (Child crouches in a ball.)
> I grew very tired, in a chrysalis I'm now found.

I rested there for two whole weeks, two whole weeks, two whole weeks. (Child stays in ball and then breaks free at end of verse.)

I rested there for two whole weeks, and one day I broke free.

Now I am a butterfly, butterfly, butterfly. (Child flies by slowly flapping her arms.)

Now I am a butterfly, flying gracefully.

Review Time

- What is the life cycle of a butterfly?
- Can you find the letters *B* and *C* in our crafts?
- What sounds do *B* as in *butterfly* and *C* as in *caterpillar* make?
- What was your favorite part of the lesson? Mine was . . .

Desert

Featured Letters: C, D, G, H, J, and S

Introductory Activity: Desert Book

Skills learned: Prereading, knowledge of the desert, reading comprehension, listening

Instructions:

1. Read aloud a book about the desert, and ask some comprehension questions.

2. Take this time to discuss how the desert is different from where you live. Or if you live in the desert, talk about how living in the desert is different from living along a coast or on a plain. Make sure you emphasize how hot and dry the desert is in the summer.

Activity 2: Saguaro Dot-to-Dot

Skills learned: Letter recognition and phonics (*S*), fine motor, prewriting, numbers, knowledge of the saguaro cactus

Materials: Construction paper, crayon

Instructions:

1. Plot dots on the construction paper in the outline of a saguaro cactus (pronounced "suh-wah-roe;" it is most commonly recognized by its large arms that reach up toward the sky). Number the dots.

2. Let your child use the crayon to connect the dots.

3. Once the saguaro has been revealed, tell her a little bit about it: Saguaros only grow about an inch a year. Some are 15 to 20 feet tall, and the ones with more than five arms are estimated to be 500 years old!

4. Make sure she knows *S* stands for *saguaro*, and have her sound it out.

Activity 3: Gila Woodpecker Holes

Skills learned: Matching, fine motor, counting, comparison, addition, subtraction, phonics (*G*)

Materials: Felt (green and black), scissors, felt board (optional)

Instructions:

1. Use the green felt to cut out two identical saguaros. (Saguaros are tall cacti with arms reaching up toward the sky.)

2. Cut 20 small black felt circles.

3. Place both saguaros on the felt board.

4. Add black circles (any number) to one of the saguaros.

5. Explain that the Gila woodpecker is a desert bird that makes a hole in the saguaro cactus to build a nest. Tell him the black circles are Gila nests.

6. Have your child count how many nests are in the saguaro.

7. Give your child extra black circles, and have him put the same number of nests on the other saguaro.

8. Put four nests on one cactus and six nests on the other. Ask your child if the saguaros have the same number of Gila nests on them. If they are not the same, ask him what he would have to do to make them the same. Repeat this with number variations.

9. Put a few nests on one cactus and have your child match the position of the nests on the other cactus.

10. Make sure your child knows that *G* stands for *Gila*, and have him make the "g" sound.

Activity 4: Cactus Colors

Skills learned: Letter recognition and phonics (*C*), colors, counting
Materials: White construction paper, 2 green crayons (different shades)
Instructions:
1. Trace a number of cacti onto the construction paper, preferably a number you are currently working on with your child. Randomly label each cactus with either an uppercase *C* or a lowercase *c*. Your child will color the uppercase *C*s one shade of green and the lowercase ones the other shade, so make a legend on the construction paper that your child can refer to.
2. Explain that a cactus is a type of plant found in the desert. Write the word "CACTUS" across the top of the construction paper. Have your child sound out the word with you and make sure he knows that C stands for *cactus*.
3. Have your child count the number of cacti on the construction paper.
4. Give him the crayons, and let him color each cactus. Make sure he follows the instructions for coloring the uppercase *C*s one color and the lowercase *c*s the other shade of green.

Activity 5: Adobe House

Skills learned: Colors, textures, letter recognition and phonics (*H*)
Materials: Construction paper, brown paint, white paint, paintbrush, sand
Instructions:
1. Draw the outline of an adobe house on the construction paper.

2. Ask your child what she thinks will happen when you mix brown paint with white paint. Will it be a darker brown, a lighter brown, or a different color entirely?

3. Add a little brown paint to the white paint. Let her mix it and see the results.

4. Add a little sand to the paint mixture, and let her mix it together.

5. Let her paint the house with the mixture.

6. Ask her what she thinks the house will feel like when it dries. Will it be smooth or scratchy? Why will it be scratchy?

7. Write the word "HOUSE" across the top of the page. Sound out the letter *H*, and have your child do the same.

Activity 6: Jackrabbit Ears

Skills learned: Large and fine motor, letter recognition and phonics (*J*), writing, dramatic play

Materials: Brown construction paper or large brown grocery bag, children's safety scissors, glue, pipe cleaners, pencil or crayon

Instructions:

1. Draw the outline of long jackrabbit ears on the construction paper.

2. Let your child cut out the ears with the safety scissors.

3. Let your child cut out a strip of construction paper that is long enough to fit around his head.

4. Explain that *J* stands for *jackrabbit*. Let him write letter *J*s on the strip of paper.

5. Have your child glue the ears to the long strip of paper.

6. Instead of gluing, taping, or stapling the headpiece together, poke the chenille piping through the ends of the long strip and adjust the paper to your child's head.

7. Let your child hop around the house like a jackrabbit!

Activity 7: Desert Snack

Skills learned: Imagination, fine motor
Materials: Graham crackers, green yogurt or prepared green pudding, sealable food storage bag
Instructions:
1. Have your child pretend she is going to have cactus yogurt or pudding. Since the desert is dry and dusty, the snack should be topped with a little "sand."
2. Place a graham cracker in the bag and seal it.
3. Have your child pound on the bag until the graham cracker looks like sand.
4. Let her pinch a little "sand" onto the top of her tasty snack. Enjoy!

Activity 8: Musical Landscape

Skills learned: Large motor, desert plant identification, dramatic play, letter recognition and phonics
Materials: Pictures of different desert plants, masking tape, music, printer paper, black marker
Instructions:
1. Find pictures of different desert plants (e.g., barrel cactus, cholla, prickly pear, saguaro, ocotillo, palo verde tree) on the Internet.
2. Tape the pictures in a circle on the floor of your family room.
3. Below each picture, tape a piece of printer paper. The printer paper should have a large letter written in marker. The letter should be the first letter for the desert plant above it. For example, if there is a picture of an ocotillo, then the printer paper below the picture should have a large letter O.
4. Let your child wear his jackrabbit ears and hop around the pictures while you play music. When the music stops, he should iden-

tify the picture and its matching letter that are closest to him. Make sure he sounds out the letter. You'll have to help him out until he learns all the plants.

Activity 9: Cactus Comparison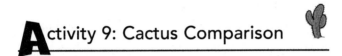

Skills learned: Counting, comparison, measurement
Materials: Tape measure
Instructions:

1. Explain to your child that the saguaro cactus only grows an inch (2.54 cm) a year. Ask him how many inches tall he would be if he only grew an inch a year.

2. Take out the tape measure, and show him what 4 inches (or whatever his age is) looks like. Help him measure where 4 inches from the ground comes on his leg. Do the same for his arm.

3. Put a number of objects on the table, and let him measure their height. Say he measures a stuffed animal that is 7 inches (18 cm) high. Then you would explain that if it were a saguaro it would be seven years old.

4. Tell him your age, and let him measure out on your legs how tall you would be if you were a saguaro cactus.

Activity 10: Desert Sunset

Skills learned: Fine motor, phonics (*S*)
Materials: Light blue or light pink construction paper; brown construction paper; children's safety scissors; crayons (red, pink, purple, yellow, orange), watercolors, or chalk
Instructions:

1. Explain that one of the more brilliant things found in the desert is the desert sunset. The colors at dusk streak beautifully through the sky. Take this time to talk about the sunset and what it means. Make sure your child knows that *S* stands for *sunset*, and have her make an *S* sound.

2. Draw simple mountain shapes on the brown construction paper. Have your child cut them out.

3. Let your child glue the mountains on the blue construction paper.

4. Give her the crayons, watercolors, or chalk, and let her make her own beautiful sunset by streaking the colors across the desert sky on the construction paper.

Activity 11: Cactus Prickles

Skills learned: Fine motor

Materials: Construction paper, dried spaghetti, flat-tip tweezers (optional)

Instructions:

1. Draw several different kinds of cacti on the construction paper.

2. Give the dried spaghetti to your child, and let him break it into small pieces (make sure he knows not to eat it!).

3. Let him glue the spaghetti onto the cacti as spines.

Variation:

For a greater challenge, let your child use tweezers to pick up the spaghetti pieces and place them on the cacti.

Activity 12: Desert Sand

Skills learned: Letter recognition and phonics (*D*), fine motor, prewriting

Materials: Jelly-roll pan, sand, glue (optional), construction paper (optional)

Instructions:

1. Pour sand in the bottom of the pan. Pour just enough to cover the bottom of the pan.

2. Explain to your child that *D* stands for *desert*. Make sure your child sounds out the letter *D* with you. Show your child how to make a letter *D*.

3. Let your child practice writing letter *D*s in the sand with his finger.

4. Let your child practice other letters and numbers in the sand, and then let him draw freely.

Variation:

1. For another way to do the activity, have your child use glue to make a large uppercase *D* and a large lowercase *d* on the construction paper. He can either make it with his finger or with a cotton-tip applicator.

2. Let your child cover the glue with sand by pinching a little sand at a time and sprinkling it onto the glue until both letters are completely covered.

3. Shake off the excess sand.

Review Time

- Is the weather in the desert hot or cold?
- Can you name some desert plants?
- Where does the Gila woodpecker make its nest?
- Can you find the letters *D, G, H, J,* and *S* in our crafts?
- What sounds do *G* as in *Gila* and *J* in *jackrabbit* make?
- What was your favorite part of the lesson? Mine was . . .

Lesson 28

Health and Nutrition

Featured Letters: F, T, V, and X

Introductory Activity: Book About Going to the Doctor

Skills learned: Prereading, familiarity with health and nutrition, reading comprehension, listening

Instructions:

1. Read aloud a book about visiting the doctor, and ask your child some comprehension questions.

2. Take this time to discuss the different doctors your child may visit and why the visits are important. You should also talk about nutrition. List some foods for your child to tell you if they are healthy foods or junk foods.

Activity 2: Toothbrush Bristles

Skills learned: Counting, number recognition, fine motor

Materials: Felt, fabric interfacing, or construction paper (white and any color), felt board (optional), black marker

Instructions:

1. Cut several toothbrush shapes (any color) out of the felt, fabric interfacing, or construction paper, omitting the bristles.

2. Use the marker to label each toothbrush with a different number. Make sure you use numbers you are currently working on with your child.

3. Cut multiple white bristles (small rectangles) from the felt, fabric interfacing, or construction paper.

4. Invite your child up to the felt board. Have her identify the number on each toothbrush and add the corresponding number of bristles. For example, if a toothbrush has a number 8 on it, your child has to place eight bristles on the toothbrush.

Variation:

1. For another way to do the activity, cut out multiple toothbrushes and draw the bristles on the toothbrush. Each toothbrush should match another toothbrush with the same number of bristles. For example, if you draw nine bristles on a toothbrush, another toothbrush should also have nine bristles.

2. Give half the toothbrushes to your child, and have her take one toothbrush at a time and count out the bristles, go to the felt board, and find the matching toothbrush.

Activity 3: Toothbrush Painting

Skills learned: Large and fine motor, knowledge of dental care
Materials: White construction paper, toothbrush, light-blue paint
Instructions:

1. Cut out a large tooth from the construction paper.

2. Explain to your child the importance of proper brushing. Take this time to discuss how food is important to the body, but food left in the teeth can cause damage. Tell her she should brush her teeth after each meal to ensure having healthy gums and teeth. Also tell her that when brushing, she should make small circles.

3. Give her the toothbrush and light-blue paint (toothpaste), and let her brush the tooth by making only small circles. The entire tooth should be covered.

Activity 4: Happy Tooth, Sad Tooth

Skills learned: Knowledge of nutrition, understanding of what foods are good or bad for teeth, letter recognition and phonics (*T*), writing

Materials: Large construction paper, food magazines, children's safety scissors, glue

Instructions:

1. Draw a line down the center of the construction paper. On the left side of the paper, draw a tooth with a happy face, and on the right side, draw a tooth with a sad face.

2. Take this time to discuss what happens to teeth if a person eats too much sugar and doesn't brush enough. Explain that all foods can do damage to teeth if a person doesn't brush and floss, but foods with high amounts of sugar can cause cavities faster.

3. Let your child flip through the food magazine and pick out healthy foods and sugary foods. Let her cut them out and glue them to the construction paper. Healthy foods make happy teeth, sugary foods make sad teeth!

4. Make sure your child know that *T* stands for *teeth*. Have her sound out the letter *T*. Let her practice writing the letter *T* on the construction paper.

Activity 5: The Many Colors of Teeth

Skills learned: Logic, familiarity with food colors and their effect on teeth

Materials: White coffee filters, colored liquids (cold tea, cola, cold coffee, punch)

Instructions:

1. Cut out several teeth from the coffee filters.

2. Explain to your child the importance of brushing teeth after each meal. You will demonstrate what can occur when teeth are not frequently brushed by soaking the coffee-filter teeth in different colored liquids.

3. Place the liquids in bowls or cups, and talk about the different colors of the liquids with your child. Ask her to identify each color. Ask her what she thinks will happen if these liquids frequently cover teeth without getting brushed off. What will happen to the coffee filters?

4. Give your child the teeth, and let her soak them in the different liquids.

5. Keep checking the teeth, and watch as they change colors. Reinforce the importance of brushing teeth.

Activity 6: Restaurant

Skills learned: Dramatic play, memory, manners, life skills

Materials: Play food or pictures from magazines

Instructions:

1. Pretend to be in a restaurant with your child. Take turns being the customer and waiter or cook.

2. The customer orders food (use play food or cut out different food items from a magazine), and the waiter has to remember what the customer ordered and deliver the food to the customer.

3. Some magazine cutouts should show nutritious foods while others present foods that are not so healthy. To reinforce a nutritional diet, make sure your child only orders healthy foods.

Activity 7: Fruit and Vegetable Relay

Skills learned: Large motor, sorting, letter recognition and phonics (*F* and *V*), writing

Materials: Food magazine, 2 pieces of construction paper, pencil

Instructions:

1. Write a large letter *F* on one piece of construction paper and a large letter *V* on the other piece of construction paper.

2. Draw a handwriting practice line on both pieces of construction paper.

3. Cut out several pictures of fruits and vegetables, and place them in a pile.

4. Make sure your child know that *F* stands for *fruit* and *V* stands for *vegetable*. Have her sound out the letters *F* and *V*.

5. Have your child practice writing her *F*s and *V*s on the handwriting practice lines.

6. Designate a place in your house for the construction-paper sheet with the *V* on it and a separate place for the construction-paper sheet with the *F* on it.

7. Have your child sort the fruits and vegetables as fast as she can by picking up a picture, determining if it is a fruit or vegetable, and bringing the picture to the appropriate place in the house.

Variation:

For another way to do the activity, you may also want to play this game with real fruits and vegetables. This way, your child will be able to see, touch, and sample each item.

ctivity 8: Adhesive Bandage Sort

Skills learned: Sorting, patterns, fine motor
Materials: 1 box of adhesive bandages (various shapes and sizes)
Instructions:
1. Empty the box of bandages, and have your child sort them according to shape and size.
2. For a greater challenge, use different shapes and sizes to make a simple pattern out of the bandages on construction paper. Have your child use the adhesive bandages to follow the pattern. Let her open them and stick them onto the paper.

ctivity 9: Doctor Role Play

Skills learned: Knowledge of doctors and what to expect at a doctor visit, dramatic play
Instructions:
1. Take turns pretending to be the doctor and the patient. Check each other's eyes, ears, and nose, and listen to each other's hearts.
2. By this time in your child's life, she has probably visited the doctor a handful of times. Some doctor visits may have been really easy, while others may not have been the best experiences. Take this time to discuss the importance of seeing the doctor and emphasize that

the doctor is available to help people who don't feel well. Keep the conversation upbeat and positive so as not to scare your child.

Activity 10: X-Ray Writing

Skills learned: Knowledge of x-rays and bones, letter recognition and phonics (*X*), fine motor, writing
Materials: White construction paper, children's safety scissors, pencil
Instructions:
1. Draw a large bone shape from the white construction paper. Draw a handwriting practice line and a sample letter *X* on the bone.
2. Take this time to discuss what bones are. Have your child tell you the different bones in her body. Explain that when a bone gets hurt or broken, the doctor will want to take a picture of it. This is called taking an x-ray. The dentist will also get a picture, or x-ray, of her teeth to make sure they are healthy.
3. Have your child cut out the bone with safety scissors.
4. Show your child the letter *X*, and have her sound it out.
5. Let her practice writing *X*s on the handwriting practice line.

Activity 11: Medicine Dropper Guessing

Skills learned: Counting, logic, fine motor, prediction
Materials: 1 medicine dropper, 1 medicine cup
Instructions:
1. Let your child guess how many full droppers of water it will take to fill a medicine cup.
2. Have her fill the medicine cup using the dropper, and be sure you count along.

3. If your child is a really good counter, have her both guess and count the number of drops it would take to fill the cup.

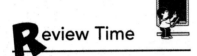

Review Time

- Can you name some healthy foods? Unhealthy?
- Can you find the letters *F*, *V*, and *X* in our activities?
- Is an apple a fruit or a vegetable? How about a banana? Green bean? Corn?
- What happens to our teeth if we don't brush properly?
- How do doctors and dentists help us?
- What was your favorite part of the lesson? Mine was . . .

Lesson 29

A B C D E F G H I J K L M N O P Q R S T U V W X Y Z

Bugs

Featured Letters: A, G, L, S, and Z

Introductory Activity: Bug Book

Skills learned: Prereading, knowledge of bugs, listening, reading comprehension

Instructions:

1. Read aloud a bug book to your child, and ask your child comprehension questions about the story.

2. Have him name all the bugs he can think of.

Activity 2: Buggy, Buggy!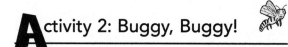

Skills learned: Ordering, counting, visual discrimination, rhyming

Materials: Construction paper, masking tape, crayons, scissors, felt board

Instructions:

1. Draw or print from your computer eight to twelve identical bug bodies. Give some of the bugs six legs, and the rest of the bugs more or less legs. Cut them out, and put masking tape behind them.

2. Explain to your child that true bugs have six legs.

3. Display the bugs on a felt board for your child. Ask him to find the true bugs by looking for bugs with six legs. You can also recite this rhyme:

Buggy, Buggy

Buggy, buggy, where are you? How do I find you? Here is a clue.

You have six legs, so I will see, if I can find you, little buggy!

4. Now remove all but one of the six-legged bugs, and have your child order the remaining bugs from fewest legs to most legs.

Activity 3: Bug Eyes

Skills learned: Creativity, dramatic play, fine and large motor, patterning (optional)

Materials: Nonplastic egg carton, pipe cleaners, glue, scissors, washable paint, decorations (extra-large sequins, glitter glue, or glitter), hole punch

Instructions:

1. Prepare the egg carton by removing the top and cutting out pairs of egg sections from the bottom. Cut a hole in the very bottom of each egg section for your child to see through. Also, you may want to paint the outside of the egg sections.

2. Give your child an egg-section pair, and help him decorate the eyes with sequins, glitter glue, or glitter.

3. Have your child wrap a pipe cleaner around a finger or pencil to make it a spring.

4. Punch a hole at the top of each eye, and insert a pipe-cleaner spring in each hole to make antennae.

5. Punch a hole on each side of the bug eyes to attach half of a pipe cleaner. Wrap the pipe cleaners over your child's ears, so he can wear the bug eyes like eyeglasses. Now get buggy!

Variation:

For a greater challenge, make Step 2 a patterning activity. For example, have your child glue the sequins into a pattern of blue, blue, green, blue, blue, green from left to right.

Activity 4: Ladybug Puppet

Skills learned: Creativity, counting, letter recognition and phonics (*L*), shapes, colors, fine and large motor, knowledge of body parts, rhyming, rhythm

Materials: Child's black glove or black adult sock; small, red, plastic disposable plate; black slick paint or paint pen; scissors; glue (may need hot glue or extra-tacky glue for good adhesion); red or black pipe cleaners; large, white pom-poms or cotton balls; google eyes, glitter glue, slick paint (optional); hole punch

Instructions:

1. Cut the red plate in half. Slip some cardboard into the glove or sock. This will keep glue from seeping through. Position the plate upside down on top of the glove or sock by holding the plate pieces together to look like a plate and then spreading out the bottom of the plate pieces. Glue on the top ends of the plate about 3 inches (7.50 cm) from the tip of the glove or sock. This causes the red plate to look like ladybug wings.

2. Discuss with your child that *ladybug* starts with an *L*. Repeat the "l" sound and then help him write an *L* on the wings.

3. Help your child paint dots on the ladybug wings. Choose a number that your child is working on, and have him paint that number of dots.

4. Glue the white pom-poms or cotton balls to the head end of the ladybug to form eyes.

5. Hole punch the plate at the head. Have your child twist the pipe cleaners around his finger or a pen to make springs and then wrap them into the holes to make antennae. Let the puppet dry.

6. Have him slip the puppet onto his hand and follow along with the song, making his ladybug do as the ladybug in the song is doing.

> *Ladybug, Ladybug (to the tune of "I'm a Little Teapot")*
> Ladybug, ladybug, flying around. You land on my hand and then
>   on the ground.
> When I try to catch you, I can see that you have landed on my
>   knee.
>
> Ladybug, ladybug, watch you go. You land on the end of my
>   elbow.
> You fly off again, and I can't see you. Oh, no! You've landed on
>   my shoe.
>
> Ladybug, ladybug, shiny and red. You fly through the air and
>   stop on my head.
> Slowly you crawl down onto my ear, then fall to the shoulder
>   that is near.
>
> Ladybug, ladybug, you tickle me so. I'll be sad to see you go.
> You crawl to my finger, then fly away. I hope to see you again
>   some day.

Activity 5: Bees Say "Buzz"

Skills learned: Writing, letter recognition and phonics (*Z*), fine motor

Materials: Yellow construction paper, children's safety scissors, black crayon

Instructions:

1. Draw a large oval onto the paper. Use the black crayon to make it look like a bumblebee. When you draw in the black stripes, set them at least 1½ inches (3.5 cm) apart.

2. Give your child the bumblebee picture, and have him cut it out.

3. Ask him what sound a bumblebee makes. What sound does *buzz* end in?

4. Have him practice writing his *Z*s in the blank stripes of the bumblebee.

Activity 6: Shoe-Box Bugs

Skills learned: Letter recognition and phonics (*A*, *G*, *L*, *S*), number recognition, fine motor, counting

Materials: Shoe box or other small box, clothespins, construction paper, glue, black marker, crayons

Instructions:

1. Cover the box with the construction paper. Then, with the open side of the box up, draw a different type of bug on each side in groups of different numbers (e.g., five ants, eight spiders, six lady bugs, and four grasshoppers). Label four clothespins with the beginning letter of each bug's name and another four clothespins with the number of bugs in each group. For the preceding example, you would make clothespins labeled *A*, *S*, *L*, *G*, 5, 8, 6, and 4. Throw all of the clothespins into the box.

2. Have your child pick a side of the box to start with. Ask him to name the type of bug he sees; then decide together what letter the bug's name starts with. Have him find the correct lettered clothespin and clip it onto the side of the box.

3. Now have him count the bugs and find the correct numbered clothespin. Have him clip it onto the box.

4. Continue with each of the box sides. Be sure to let him do the pinching of the clothespins.

Activity 7: Order the Bumblebees

Skills learned: Ordering, counting
Materials: Construction paper, glue, black marker, scissors
Instructions:

1. Cut four to ten ovals out of construction paper (about 3 by 1½ inches long [8 by 4 cm]). Decorate them as bumblebees (face, wings, and legs), but leave off the stripes.

2. Now draw on the stripes, adding one stripe for each bee you make. For example, if you cut out five bees, the first bee would have one stripe, the second bee would have two stripes, the third bee would have three stripes, and so on. For older children, use larger numbers.

3. Give your child the bees, and have him glue them onto construction paper in consecutive order, counting up or down.

Activity 8: I Spy a Bug

Skills learned: Visual discrimination
Materials: Index cards, multiple bug stickers (various kinds of bugs)
Instructions:

1. From the bug stickers, choose three to four different bugs to be the I-spy bugs.

2. Stick different numbers of each kind of I-spy bug onto an index card—for example, two ants, four lady bugs, three beetles. Disguise the I-spy bugs by placing different bug stickers around them and partially covering them.

3. To make a key card, stick one example of each I-spy bug onto another index card, and write the number of times each appears on the jumbled card.

4. Give your child the jumbled card and key, and have him find the I-spy bugs.

Activity 9: Beetle Race

Skills learned: Large motor

Instructions:

1. Have your child sit on his bottom and place his hands and feet on the floor. Have him lift his bottom up (to look like a beetle). Show him how to move his hands and feet to walk like a bug.

2. Make start and finish lines, and have him race you or another child.

Activity 10: Where Are the Bugs?

Skills learned: Knowledge of bugs, visual discrimination, letter or number recognition, fine and large motor

Materials: Card stock, clothespins, scissors, markers

Instructions:

1. Draw or print from your computer a number of bugs on the card stock. Cut them out, and hide them outside or around your house. Use clothespins to attach them to their hiding place.

2. Have your child find the hidden bugs.

3. Make sure your child squeezes the clothespins to release the bugs.

Variation:

For a greater challenge, you could also write a letter, shape, or number on the back of each bug for your child to identify.

Activity 11: Bug Memory

Skills learned: Memory, knowledge of bugs

Materials: 4 to 10 index cards, bug stickers or color markers, scissors

Instructions:

1. Cut the index cards in half. Make pairs of memory cards by drawing identical bugs on each half of a card. You can also use identical bug stickers. Each pair of cards should be different from the other pairs (e.g., 2 grasshoppers, 2 ladybugs, 2 beetles, 2 ants). If you run out of different types of bugs, vary their colors.

2. Show your child the memory cards, and turn them over in rows.

3. Let your child turn over two cards. If they match, he gets to keep them. If they do not match, encourage him to memorize where they are and turn them back over.

4. You go next. Continue play until all the cards have been matched. The player with the most matches wins.

Activity 12: Grasshopper Hopscotch

Skills learned: Large and fine motor, number recognition, hand-eye coordination, following directions

Materials: Sidewalk chalk (or masking tape), grasshopper painted on a rock or a bug toy

Instructions:

1. Draw a hopscotch game on your driveway, or tape it out on your floor. There are various ways to draw a hopscotch game, but one variation follows in Step 3.

2. Explain to your child how to play hopscotch, and then play it with him. You may need to help him.

3. There are six rows in a hopscotch game. The first row is one square numbered 1. The second row is two squares numbered 2 and 3. The third row is one square numbered 4, and so on, until you reach the last row of two squares numbered 8 and 9.

4. Your child must throw his stone on the square marked 1. Your child will jump up the hopscotch by hopping on one foot in the single squares and on two feet in the double squares. He must skip the square with the stone in it. When he jumps back down the hopscotch, he picks up the stone on his way. A second turn is the same except that the stone is thrown on the 2, and so on.

Variation:

For a lesser challenge, just emphasize naming the numbers as he jumps, throwing the stone to the correct number, and jumping with one and two feet.

Review Time

- How many legs does a true bug have?
- Can you find the letters *A, G, L, S,* and *Z* in our activities?
- What sounds do *L* as in *ladybug* and *Z* as in *buzz* make?
- Can you name four different bugs?
- What comes first in counting, a 5 or a 2?
- What was your favorite part of the lesson? Mine was . . .

Lesson 30

A B C D E F G H I J K L M N O P Q R S T U V W X Y Z

Summer

Featured Letters: N, S, and U

Introductory Activity: Summer Book

Skills learned: Knowledge of summer, prereading, listening, reading comprehension

Instructions:

1. Read aloud the book to your child, and ask comprehension questions about the story you read.

2. Discuss things that she does in the summer (e.g., what the weather is like or what clothes she wears).

Activity 2: Sun Fade

Skills learned: Knowledge of the sun's power, letter recognition and phonics (*S*, *U*, *N*)

Materials: Large black or navy blue construction paper; large construction-paper letter cutouts for *S*, *U*, and *N*; masking tape; any other objects that would leave an interesting shadow; sunny day

Instructions:

1. Give your child the large construction paper and the *S, U, N* letter cutouts. Have her identify the letters.

2. Place tape on the back of each letter, and stick them to the large paper.

3. Have your child choose small objects that will make interesting shadows.

4. Take the construction paper and objects outside, and lay them down in full sun where they will not be disturbed. Be sure that the letters are facing up, and place the objects securely onto the paper. If the objects are too light, tape them down.

5. Come back and check the paper a few hours later to see if the sun has faded the exposed paper. You should eventually see lighter paper around the shadows that your objects cast.

6. Discuss with your child the power of the sun, how it can fade colors, and how it can burn people's skin.

Activity 3: S'mores and Lemonade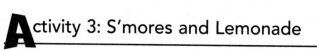

Skills learned: Fine motor, knowledge of the sun's heat, knowledge of sweet and sour, following directions, measuring, counting

Materials: 6 lemons at room temperature, sugar, large bowl, drinking pitcher, glasses, spoon, juice squeezer if available, graham crackers, chocolate bars, large marshmallows, aluminum foil, pie plate, hot and sunny day

Instructions:

1. Have your child assemble her s'more by making a sandwich out of two graham crackers, a large section of chocolate bar (ask for a specific number of rectangles and have her break them off in one chunk), and two large marshmallows.

2. Put aluminum foil inside a pie plate, and place the s'more on top of the foil.

3. Put the s'more outside to cook in the sun, and check it periodically. It is ready to eat when the chocolate and marshmallows have partially melted and the sandwich sticks together.

4. Discuss with your child the power of the sun's heat. Show how it cooked the s'more and how it can hurt people. Talk about sunscreen.

5. Slice the lemons in halves or quarters.

6. Give your child a bowl, and have her squeeze the juice out of the lemons into the container. Let her taste the lemon juice. Discuss the word *sour*.

7. When enough juice has been squeezed to make lemonade, put it into a pitcher with some water and sugar to taste. Drink this with your s'more snack later.

Activity 4: Sandy Letters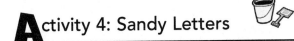

Skills learned: Letter recognition, fine motor, sense of touch, colors

Materials: White construction paper, multicolored sand, glue, pencil, cotton-tip applicator

Instructions:

1. On a sheet of construction paper, write two-dimensional letters for your child to identify.

2. Give your child the lettered paper and glue. Have her outline the letters with washable glue and spread the glue with the applicator so that the whole letter is covered.

3. Have her take pinches of colored sand and sprinkle it onto the glue.

4. Shake the excess sand into the trash or save it for later.

5. Once the glue is dry, ask your child to close her eyes. Hold her finger and trace one of the letters. Be sure to trace the letter as she would write it. Ask her if she can guess what the letter is.

Activity 5: Sunflower Tweeze

Skills learned: Fine motor, counting, number recognition, writing
Materials: A real sunflower or sunflower seeds in their shells, tweezers, yellow and another color construction paper, pencil, scissors, glue
Instructions:
1. On a sheet of construction paper, draw several sunflower centers (circles) with a different number written in each. Space the centers apart so that petals can be added later.
2. From the yellow construction paper, cut out multiple sunflower petals.
3. Give your child the paper with the numbered flower centers, a real sunflower, and tweezers. Have her tweeze out the number of sunflower seeds to match the written number of the first center and glue them down. Continue with each flower center. (If you can't find a real flower, just use a bag of sunflower seeds in their shells.)
4. Have your child glue the yellow petals around the center of each flower.
5. Have her count the seeds in each center, and help her write the number next to each flower.

Activity 6: Beach Ball Toss

Skills learned: Letter and number recognition, colors, large motor, phonics (optional), counting
Materials: Multicolored plastic blow-up beach ball, paper, pencil, masking tape

Instructions:

1. Cut out 3-by-3-inch (7.5 by 7.5 cm) squares of paper, and write a letter or number that you are working with on each. Tape the squares all around the beach ball.

2. Sit with your child and throw the beach ball to her.

3. When she catches it, ask her to identify what colors her hands are holding.

4. Ask her to identify the letter or number her hands are closest to.

5. If she has a number, ask her to do a large motor skill that number of times. For example, ask her to jump up and down five times if she lands on the 5.

6. If she has a letter, ask her to tell you the name and the sound of the letter.

Activity 7: Shadow Silhouette

Skills learned: Knowledge of self, knowledge of sun and shadow, being still

Materials: Large piece of black construction paper, children's safety scissors, large construction paper or picture matte to mount the silhouette, glue, lamp with shade removed, pencil, scissors, masking tape, chalk

Instructions:

1. Place your child on a low chair near a wall with her left shoulder toward it.

2. Shine your light on her from her right side so that you are casting a direct shadow of her silhouette onto the wall.

3. Tape the black construction paper to the wall so that it captures the shadow.

4. Have her sit very still, and trace her shadow onto the paper with a pencil. Do this twice so that each of you can cut one out.

5. Cut out the black silhouette, and mount it on an extra piece of paper or a picture matte. Write your child's name and the date at the bottom of the picture.

6. Have your child cut out the extra silhouette. You may need to trace the pencil markings with chalk so your child can see them.

Activity 8: Ice-Cube Melt Race

Skills learned: Creativity, knowledge of heat and melting
Materials: Ice cubes, sunny day (optional), various objects available to help create heat (have your child brainstorm these)
Instructions:
1. Show your child the ice cubes in a bowl, and ask her what will happen if they are left out on the counter. Discuss what makes ice melt.

2. Brainstorm with your child how you could make the ice cubes melt faster than they do on the counter (e.g., place the ice cubes outside, blow on them, put them in water, sprinkle rock salt on them).

3. Have each of you pick a method, and then race to see who can melt an ice cube the fastest.

Activity 9: Splatter Painting

Skills learned: Large motor, colors and color mixing
Materials: Nice day outside, very large butcher paper in a light color, washable tempera paints (watered down), house painting brush (best to have one for each color of paint), bowls to hold paint, tape, water hose for cleanup, smock or old swimsuits

Instructions:

1. This activity needs to be done outside. Prepare by taping butcher paper to a fence or on the ground where you won't mind getting some paint.

2. Place the watered-down paints into bowls.

3. Explain to your child that she is going to splatter paint. Demonstrate how to get some paint onto the brush and fling it onto the paper.

4. Emphasize that the paint must stay on the paper and that she should not fling it at people or other objects. She must also be careful not to fling it backward.

5. Let your child rinse the wall or fence with a water hose when she is done.

Activity 10: Squirt Tag

Skills learned: Fine and large motor, following directions, cooperation

Materials: Spray water bottles filled with water, a nonslippery spot outside, old shoes that can get wet, towels for cleanup

Instructions:

1. Dress your child, yourself, and/or other players in old swimsuits. Old shoes should be worn, too.

2. Show him how to squeeze the trigger of a water bottle to squirt it.

3. The game is to run around and try to tag one another by squirting water. You can play just to keep score based on how many times you are squirted, or someone can be IT and try to tag the other player(s).

4. Emphasize that there is no squirting in the face. Any face squirting will result in the removal of half of the offending player's water.

 **R**eview Time

- What makes ice melt?
- Why do we protect our skin from the summer sun?
- Can you find the letters *N, S,* and *U* in the activities?
- What was your favorite activity in this lesson? Mine was . . .

Index